# PARENTS ON THE SPOT!

Also in the Good Housekeeping Parent Guides Series

*Little Kids, Big Questions: Practical Answers to the Difficult Questions Children Ask About Life* by Judi Craig, Ph.D.

*Battles, Hassles, Tantrums & Tears: Strategies for Coping with Conflict and Making Peace at Home* by Susan Beekman and Jeanne Holmes

*"Wanna Be My Friend?": How to Strengthen Your Child's Social Skills* by Leanne Domash, Ph.D., with Judith Sachs

# PARENTS ON THE SPOT!

*What to Do When Kids Put You There*

Judi Craig, Ph.D.

Hearst Books
New York

**A Skylight Press book**



Published by arrangement with Skylight Press, 260 West 72nd Street, Suite 6-C, New York, N.Y. 10023.

It is the policy of William Morrow and Company, Inc., and its imprints and affiliates, recognizing the importance of preserving what has been written, to print the books we publish on acid-free paper, and we exert our best efforts to that end.

Library of Congress Cataloging-in-Publication Data

Craig, Judith E., 1940–
Parents on the spot! : what to do when kids put you there / Judi Craig.
p. cm.
Includes bibliographical references and index.
ISBN 0-688-12433-X
1. Discipline of children. 2. Problem children. 3. Child rearing. I. Title.
HQ770.4.C73 1994 93-27178
649′.64—dc20 CIP

Printed in the United States of America

First Edition

1 2 3 4 5 6 7 8 9 10

BOOK DESIGN BY LISA STOKES

to anyone who has ever taken on the most
difficult job in the world . . .
being a parent

## *About the Good Housekeeping Parent Guides*

Children are a most wonderful gift in our lives—and they are also a challenge! That's why, nine years ago, we created *Good Housekeeping*'s largest-ever special editorial section: the Child Care section. Winner of a National Magazine Award in 1988, this annual section has grown by leaps and bounds to comprise more than one hundred pages, featuring articles from such notable collaborators as the American Academy of Pediatrics and the Bank Street College of Education.

THE GOOD HOUSEKEEPING PARENT GUIDES continue this spirit of helping parents meet the challenges of childrearing. Written by uniquely qualified authorities, these lively, informative books invite you to explore in-depth the everyday challenges of parenting. They are filled with ideas, examples, and strategies drawn from the real-life situations we all encounter with children. They offer new ways to understand and respond to children, as well as guidance on handling our own needs as parents.

We hope you find these guides valuable additions to your home library, providing new insights into your children, as well as innovative ideas to consider in your role as a parent. Most of all, we hope that they contribute to the loving bond you share with your child.

John Mack Carter
Editor-in-Chief
*Good Housekeeping*

With thanks and gratitude to . . .
Meg Schneider and Lynn Sonberg at Skylight Press, and
Toni Sciarra at Hearst Books,
for their continued encouragement, thoughtful perspectives, and valuable expertise

# CONTENTS

CHAPTER 1. **THE "HOT SEAT": A PARENT'S QUANDARY** 19

CHAPTER 2. **THE DAILY ROUTINE** 43

The Morning Grump 45
The Home Wrecker 47
The Picky Eater 48
"Give Me Back My Diaper!" 50
The Bed Wetter 51
"I'll Make My BM Anywhere but in the Toilet!" 54
"I Hate Baths!" 56
"I Don't Want to Get Up!" 58
"I Don't Want to Clean Up!" 59
"I Can't Sleep!" 60
The Late Diner 62
The Kid Who Can't Shift Gears 63
"Why Can't We Do It the Old Way?" 65
"I'm Bored!" 66
"The Sitter's Mean!" 67

CHAPTER 3. **THE SOCIAL SIDE** 69

The Tattletale 70
The Poor Sport 71
"I Have a New Playmate!" (But You Can't See Her!) 72
The Ungrateful Kid 73
"But It's Not My Fault!" 74
The Car Pool Nobody Wants 75
The Thief 77
"But I Want *Designer* Jeans!" 78
"I Won't Kiss Grandma!" 79
"I Won't Play!" 80
The Kid Who Asks at the Wrong Time 81
The Restaurant Terror 82
"I've Got to Win!" 83
"Your Mom Gave You Away!" 84
The Kid Who Makes Embarrassing Remarks About Other People 85
"I'm Not Sharing This Toy with My Sister!" 86
The Child Who's Too Friendly to Strangers 88
"I Don't Like This Birthday Party!" 89
"Mr. Supersilly" 90
"But I Have to Be First!" 91
The Constant Talker 92
"I'm Not Talking!" 93
"I Don't Have Any Friends!" 94
"But They All Tease Me!" 95
The Unfriendly Host 96
"It's My Turn to Be on Your Lap!" 97

CHAPTER 4. **AGGRESSIVENESS** 99

"I Hate You!" 100
The Biter 101
The Kid Who Hits a Parent 103
The Tantrumer 104
"But I Didn't Mean to Hurt the Doggy!" 105

| | | |
|---|---|---|
| | The Destroyer | 106 |
| | "She Did It!" "He Did It!" | 108 |
| | The Taunter | 110 |
| | The Child Who Deliberately Hurts Herself | 111 |
| | "I'll Do It" (But Then I Won't!) | 112 |
| CHAPTER 5. | **SCHOOL** | 115 |
| | "Don't Leave Me Here!" | 117 |
| | "My Tummy Hurts!" | 119 |
| | "I'm Not Going!" | 120 |
| | "Will You Help Me with My Homework?" | 122 |
| | The Child Who Doesn't Pay Attention | 124 |
| | "What Homework?" | 126 |
| | "I Cheated" | 128 |
| | "I Got into a Fight!" | 130 |
| | The Underachiever with Great Potential | 133 |
| | "The Teacher's Wrong!" | 135 |
| | "I'm Suspended!" | 136 |
| CHAPTER 6. | **SEX** | 139 |
| | The Public Masturbator | 140 |
| | "What's Wrong with That Word?" | 141 |
| | The Nude Dude | 142 |
| | "Can I See?" | 143 |
| | "But I Want to Be a Girl!" | 144 |
| | "But It's Only a Magazine!" | 145 |
| | "We're Playing Doctor!" | 147 |
| | The Inappropriate Toucher | 148 |
| | "What Are You and Daddy Doing?" | 149 |
| CHAPTER 7. | **FEARS AND ANXIETIES** | 151 |
| | "But I Saw a Monster!" | 152 |
| | The Night Screamer | 153 |
| | "But I Didn't Make 100!" | 155 |
| | The Midnight Intruder | 156 |

"I Want to Marry Daddy!" 158
"Who Do You Love the Most?" 159
"But That's Not Fair!" 160
"But You Wouldn't Let Me Have That When I Was That Age!" 161
"No, I'm Not Sick!" 162
"I Have Bad Thoughts!" 163
The Dreamer 164
The Curious Adoptee 165
"I Won't Stay Here Without You!" 166
"I Can't Do Anything Right!" 167

CHAPTER 8. **OPPOSITIONAL BEHAVIOR** 169

The Uncontainable Spirit! 169
The Tuner-Outer 172
The Kid Who's Never Satisfied 173
The Whiner 174
The Negative Child 175
The Kid Who Has to Have the Last Word 177
The Child Who Lies 177

CHAPTER 9. **THREATS AND CHALLENGES** 181

"You Can't Catch Me!" 182
"You Can't Make Me!" 183
"I'm Not Kissing You Ever Again!" 184
"So Who Cares, Anyway?" 185
"You Don't Love Me!" 185
"You'll Be Sorry!" 186
"I'll Run Away!" 187
"I'll Kill Myself!" 188

CHAPTER 10. **FAMILY PROBLEMS** 191

"Please Don't Fight!" 191
The Innocent Blunderer 193
The Family Secret Teller 194
"How Can You Do That to Me?" 195

"What Do You Mean There's No Money?" 196
"Dad, Mommy Was Drunk!" 197
"But It's Okay with Dad!" 198
"Can't You Please Get Along?" 199
"I Want a New Daddy!" 200
"I Don't Want to Go See Daddy!" 201

CHAPTER 11. **JUST A MINUTE! THAT'S *MY* CHILD!** 205
The Misinformed Teacher 206
The Problem Teacher 207
The Unwelcome Disciplinarian 207
The Upset Neighbor 208
"I Didn't Do It!" 209
"But I Don't Believe That!" 210

**SUGGESTED READINGS** 211

**INDEX** 217

# PARENTS ON THE SPOT!

# CHAPTER 1

## *The "Hot Seat": A Parent's Quandary*

Kids, even the best of them, are predictably unpredictable. Just when you think you and your child have ironed out the "kinks," along comes another quandary to jolt you into the "hot seat":

> Your five-year-old son looks around the deli and not so quietly exclaims, "Why is that lady so fat?"
>
> Your darling four-year-old daughter is given a present by your boss, rips off the paper, and says, "Yuck, I don't like this!"
>
> Your eight-year-old Little Leaguer comes home utterly filthy after a muddy practice and announces, "I'm not taking a bath and you can't make me!"
>
> You're eating dinner at a nice restaurant and as the waiter is tossing your salads, your six-year-old suddenly asks, "Daddy, what's a condom?"

Or maybe you're faced with a situation that's been going on for a while; for example, your child might be giving you grief about doing her homework. You've tried patience and understanding, lectures and threats, maybe even swats on your little one's behind. You feel your patience wearing thin. Then it happens: perhaps a sassy remark, a call from the teacher, a disappointing grade on a report card. Whatever it is, you've suddenly had it. You feel as if you're on the "hot seat" again. The urge to do something, *anything,* overtakes you. But what?

Even if you're normally a laid-back, in-control person, such scenarios can plummet you into a state of confusion. It is amazing to you that such a small being can wreak such havoc with your ability to cope. So, it's important and reasonable to ask what is getting to you at these moments.

## WHY THE "HOT SEAT" SENSATION?

You might see your child's behavior as evidence that you're a lousy parent and that, somewhere along the line, you missed the boat. And if you don't blame yourself, you might fear that your mother, spouse, neighbor, or mother-in-law probably will! If the "hot seat" incident occurs in public, you might even find yourself suddenly worrying about what complete strangers think of your parenting ability.

You might also wonder if something is drastically wrong with your child, or worry that he's going to turn out to confirm your worst fears. You might notice some trait or characteristic in him that reminds you of a negative trait in yourself, and you desperately want to spare him the painful feelings and consequences you suffered as a result of it.

"Where did I go wrong?" you wonder as you try to handle feelings of fury, confusion, frustration, hurt, guilt, humiliation, and/or helplessness. After all, you have the best of intentions. You love your child, you teach her right from wrong, you chauffeur her to softball, ballet and piano lessons, you provide what she needs and most of what she wants, you try to explain things to her calmly, you sacrifice God-knows-what for her, you tell her she's the best kid in the world, and you give her your wisest advice and guidance. So why is she like this?

## WHY DO KIDS DO THESE THINGS?

Children don't have the experience, wisdom, or cognitive ability of adults. Depending on their ages, they have differing capacities for understanding what's socially appropriate and polite. They also tend to be more honest than adults about what they think and feel, expressing themselves candidly with a bluntness that can make adults shudder.

Kids also love to test adults. Sometimes that means being shocking, or even downright defiant. They might be acting up to grab some extra attention or to see if you can be counted on to be consistent in your limit setting.

Children, like adults, can also have a bad day. Their needs can suddenly change because of something that's happened. For instance, you might have a child who never balks when you leave him with his favorite sitter. Then one night he surprises you by frantically protesting and clinging to you as you try to leave because he saw a scary movie earlier that afternoon.

## STRATEGIES FOR SANE PARENTING

You might like to refresh your memory about some parenting "basics" for disciplining your child. In this case, "discipline" is defined as training that develops self-control and personal character, and it includes a parent's use of positive strategies as well as negative consequences.

Why is discipline so important? Why do we need to set limits and boundaries for our youngsters? The answer goes far beyond wanting to keep an orderly household or to have appropriate control over our children.

When a child grows up in a home with few or no limits, several problems can arise. She might feel that her parents are letting her have her own way simply because they don't have the energy or inclination to deal with her, which translates into "They really don't care about me." If she is indulged and experiences no limits, she might grow up to be an egocentric, demanding person who has no frustration tolerance and is easily bored. She expects the world to bend to her needs and to provide stimulation, excitement, and creature comforts for her just as her parents did. Lack of structure at home also leads to unpredictability, and a child needs predictability in order to feel secure. She likes to know, deep down, that her parents are in control so she can put her energy into learning and relating.

Of course, the flip side is the child who is raised in a home that is too strict, coercive, or punitive. If she experiences too many rules, parental inflexibility, and/or an endless stream of anxious reminders, depending on her personality, she's likely to grow up to be either highly insecure and dependent or very rebellious.

The basic purpose of parental discipline is to help a child to internalize limits and develop self-discipline. She'll feel good about herself and her capabilities, and she'll also be able to empathize with other people's needs. She'll take appropriate responsibility for herself without blaming other people for her problems. She'll be able to plan and to accomplish goals without having unnecessary anxiety about being perfect.

Remember that the most important factor in using any particular strategy with your child is that *you* feel comfortable with it. After all, every youngster is different. What works beautifully for one child might be a disaster for another. And something your best friend does with her child might not suit your or your child's temperament at all.

Realize too that a "perfect parent" has never existed. So give up the fantasy that you can ever be totally and completely consistent, rational, or calm. Of course you'll yell, lose your cool, say things you wish you could take back, be too strict, be too lenient, and get fed up. After all you are a human being—so be gentle with yourself. What's important is that you make that emotional connection with your child that allows him to know that you really do love and care about him no matter what!

## Praise

Every parent knows that liberal doses of praise go a long way toward helping a child develop high self-esteen. But praise does even more—it results in a more cooperative child. Many behavior problems begin because parents pay more attention to what their children do *wrong* than to what they do *right!*

It's easy to compliment a youngster when he successfully does what you've asked him to do. The problem is that many parents praise only on the *condition* that their kids perform in specific ways. Getting A's on report cards, remembering to feed the dog, hanging up the bathroom towels, taking dishes to the sink—these are things most parents will notice and comment on if they're aware of the importance of praise. But this conditional kind of praise can be earned only by the child's *doing* something to earn it.

What is really necessary for a youngster to have high self-esteem is to know that a parent values him for his *essence*—for being a unique human being without necessarily having to *do* anything. Even if he's making bad grades, wetting his bed, writing on the walls, refusing to clean his hamster cage, talking back (or any number of things kids do that drive parents up the wall), he still needs to know he's loved and valued.

How can you give him this important *unconditional* praise? Simply let him know you enjoy being around him. You might say something like "Honey, I'm sure glad you rode to the store with me. I really like having your company," or "It's really fun when we make cookies together," or "You're a really neat kid! Did you know that?" or "You know, honey, you're just the kind of little girl I always wanted to have."

You also can focus on your child's *qualities* rather than on her *actions*. Examples would be statements like "Boy! You really have a great sense of humor!" or "You know, I've noticed that you're really good with animals. I think it's because you're so gentle and caring," or "I really like the way you think about other people's feelings, Tommy. You're a very thoughtful person," or "Honey, when you were talking with your friend yesterday I realized you're a really good listener. People feel comfortable with you, and that's very important."

Another way to convey acceptance and love to your child without her having to do anything to earn it is to give her physical affection.

Whether it's a kiss, a hug, or a pat on the head as you walk past her, touch is a powerful way to let a child (or an adult!) know you care. Of course some kids will act as if they couldn't care less about "all that mushy stuff." While it's important to respect your child's individual preferences about the kind of affection he prefers, be sure to hang in there and find some way to make physical contact. For example, some parents will negotiate "just one hug a day to humor good-old Dad." Some youngsters will tolerate a five-minute neck or back rub ("but no kisses, please, Mom!").

Giving your youngster physical affection as well as conditional and unconditional praise will not mean that you won't have hassles with him (or times when you'll feel like wringing his neck!). But you are more likely to experience fewer problems with your child because whatever disciplinary measures do occur, he'll know deep down that you love him and think he's pretty terrific.

### Talking and Listening

All parents want to have good communication with their child. But sometimes the harder a parent tries to "communicate," the faster the child tunes out!

The fact is that many parents don't talk with kids—they talk *at* them, lecturing or arguing. A child asks a question and the parent responds with too much information, not pausing to check whether or not the child understands what has already been said, much less whether the child wants to know more. The more the youngster's eyes glaze over, the more (and the louder) the parent continues. The parent, of course, justifies her behavior by saying that she's only trying to get her point across.

When a parent complains that a child is argumentative, you can be sure someone else in the family (probably that parent!) also argues. After all, a person can't argue with herself! Somebody else has to be participating too. The parent who gets caught up in arguing often feels that it's important to "have the last word" with a child. In truth having the "last word" means nothing; what counts is the *leverage* a parent has. It's the parent who has final say about such matters as television and phone privileges, bedtime, having friends visit, and so on.

It's also important to remember to talk to kids in positive terms. Rather than saying, "If you don't do your homework by seven o'clock, you won't see any television tonight!" you could say, "If you get your homework done by seven o'clock, you can watch television tonight!" This simple difference in approach is likely to result in a difference in degree of cooperation!

Also watch your use of the word "don't!" Why? Because the brain can't translate the "don't" until it first translates the rest of the sentence! For instance, if I tell you, "Don't think about a purple giraffe!" the next thing you'll think about is a purple giraffe! Now think about a situation where a parent walks outside and finds her eight-year-old walking on the edge of the roof. In an effort to keep the child safe while she finds a way to get the child down from the roof, a parent might unthinkingly shout something like "Don't go too close to the edge!" rather than "Move back! You're too close to the edge!"

The truth is that the word "don't" also tends to mobilize resistance. People, including children, don't like being told they can't do something; consequently, the rebellious side of them gets hooked with "don'ts." If I now tell you, "Don't read the rest of this chapter!" for example, you'd be tempted to read on even if you had been planning to put the book down right after reading this paragraph!

Closely related to talking is yelling, something most parents and kids will do at some point. Parents who yell a lot often feel very guilty about it, not realizing that they have unwittingly taught their kids not to obey *until* Mom or Dad yells!

What happens is something like this: A parent asks a child to do something, but the child doesn't comply. The parent asks again. At some point—maybe after two requests, maybe after ten—the parent gets fed up with the child's noncompliance and yells, "That's it! If you don't do this right this minute you'll have no television tonight," or "You do this now or you're going to your room for a time-out!" The child then does what's been requested and the parent asks himself for the umpteenth time why on earth he has to yell to get his kid to mind.

The truth is, it wasn't the yelling that really did the trick—it was the fact that the parent set a consequence. If the parent had set that consequence after the first request, chances are the yelling need not have occurred! The parent who acts earlier in the game (rather than just talking) will not feel the buildup of frustration that so often leads to yelling.

Of course, the other half of "good communication" is the fine art of listening. Many parents only half-listen to their youngsters, saying, "Uh-huh," or "So what happened?" while being preoccupied with their own thoughts. It is much better to tell a child that you can't really listen at the moment and to save the conversation for a little later, rather than to *pretend* to listen. Even though they might be impatient about having to wait, kids begin to appreciate how nice it is to have parents who will give their undivided attention when the conversation occurs.

The other mistake parents make when listening to their children is to jump in immediately with an explanation, opinion, suggestion, analysis, or criticism. It's much better to hang back a little and reflect the child's feeling or ask for more information. Statements like "Gee, you sound pretty upset. Tell me more about that," or "What do you think went wrong?" or "Tell me why you think that, honey," encourage the child to continue talking.

This kind of listening, often called "active listening," has two advantages. First, a parent is more likely to find out what's *really* going on (as opposed to what she *thinks* is going on), and the child often comes up with his own solution to the problem, giving the parent the opportunity to praise the youngster for clear or mature thinking. Second, if the child seems "stuck," active listening makes the parent aware of this, so the parent can help the youngster work through and become more skillful at resolving the problem in the future.

Clearly, many everyday hassles with kids can be nipped in the bud, or at least minimized, by a parent's being able to talk and to listen effectively. This means keeping the lines of communication turned on in order to keep the kids from turning off!

## Negative Consequences

Before we look at some common consequences for misbehavior, let's talk about why this section isn't called "Punishment." It used to be that parents "punished" kids when they were naughty or disobedient. Now "punishment" is out and "consequences" are in.

The idea is that punishment in the old-fashioned sense included more than just a consequence: It meant that a child was supposed to feel bad about himself in addition to being given some restriction or losing some privilege. Now the emphasis is on teaching youngsters that mistakes are lessons, not signals for a moral "beating up on oneself." Parents give consequences to let a child know her *behavior* is bad and not to make her feel that *she* is bad.

Also, punishment is often unrelated to the crime. In contrast, consequences are usually logically linked to the child's behavior (a morning dawdler might be sleepy, so she'll need to go to bed earlier).

Let's take a look at some of the common consequences parents use.

### *Spanking*

Most parenting experts do not recommend spanking (or any negative physical touching such as ear pulling, shaking, pinching, and so on) as a discipline method. (However many, including myself, do feel that an *occasional* swift swat on the behind to make a point about a dangerous situation, such as running out into the street, is okay for a preschooler.) And why has this traditional method for dealing with children's misbehavior (that is still popular with many parents) become so unpopular with the experts?

First, consider the *behavioral* message of a spanking: If you are angry with someone and/or you want to control his behavior and you are bigger and stronger than he is, you hit him. Is this really what you want to teach your child?

Second, there are many kids for whom spankings simply don't

work. In fact, spankings worsen their behavior and often make these children more aggressive both with peers and with adults.

Third, some parents who spank children are vulnerable to losing control and becoming abusive. When this happens (or when a parent *thinks* she's gone too far), the parent often feels very guilty and tries to "undo" the actual or fantasized mistreatment. She might become extremely affectionate, close, or attentive to that child after the spanking is over, perhaps even giving the youngster a treat. This kind of behavior gives the child the unhealthy message that the way to get the real "goodies" from Mommy or Daddy is to misbehave, suffer through a spanking, and *then* get lots of extra loving and affection! Also, it can send a message that the child's life isn't secure: Mom or Dad is not consistent and cannot be counted on to be emotionally stable when that parent feels scared, sad, angry, or hurt.

### *Time-out*

This is simply a time when a child is removed from social attention, of parents, siblings, or friends. A youngster can be sent for a time-out to a particular chair, a hallway, or a certain room in the house.

Some young children can be given a time-out sitting within clear view of the parent. If the child sits quietly, all is well. But many youngsters don't just sit and take their time-out without protest. They'll make noises, faces, and movements which end up getting a parent's attention—the very thing that's supposed to be taken away! It's best to send children who do this to their room or to some other acceptable room in the house.

The length of time a child spends in the time-out area need only be three to five minutes for a young child and not more than ten to thirty minutes for an older one. If a child is yelling and screaming in time-out or throwing things around the room, be sure to let her know that the minutes on the time-out clock don't start ticking away until she's calmed down.

Of course, when you first start to use this method, you may have to use time-outs frequently to help your child learn that you mean what you say. But if you're giving him more than two or three time-outs a day after the first week or so, you might want to take another look at your expectations. Perhaps you're tackling too many of your child's negative or inappropriate behaviors at once. Consider focusing on just one for the time being and let the others slide for a time. Once your child understands that you mean what you say and that you will stick to the limits you set, he won't have to test you quite so hard.

If it seems that you are having to give your child too many time-outs, you might also consider whether your youngster is experiencing some stress in his life that is contributing to his misbehavior. Obvious examples would be if you are in the midst of a divorce, if there's a new baby at home, or if you've recently moved. Addressing the underlying issue and giving your child the necessary information and/or reassurance he needs can help to lessen the behavior problems he's having.

Some parents worry that sending a youngster to her own room for time-out is not a good idea, since she'll have access to toys, books, and other entertainment possibilities. Or they'll try to keep the child from having any fun by making her sit in a certain place, lie on a bed, and so on.

However, the purpose of a time-out is to let a child know that certain behaviors are unacceptable and to show that the adult in the house intends to maintain appropriate control over the child until the child is old enough to control herself. This message doesn't mean that the child has to suffer in some way. If she starts playing and makes something positive out of a negative situation, isn't that a constructive strategy?

Monitoring your child's behavior while your youngster is in time-out also means bird-dogging your child, and paying attention to your youngster increases her negative attention-getting power. The purpose of time-out is just the opposite!

There are actually two different situations of misbehavior for which time-out can be used effectively. The first is when a child has violated some rule (stood on the coffee table, hit his sister). In this case, the parent determines the appropriate amount of time the child spends in time-out for that misbehavior.

In the second situation some ongoing behavior (whining, tantrums, inappropriate silliness) of the child that the adult wants stopped is cause for time-out. In this case, the child is told that she is to go to time-out and may join you only when she's ready to *stop* the inappropriate behavior. The point is for the youngster to learn to bring herself into control. She might go to time-out, control herself immediately, and come right back to her original place. Or she might stay in the room a very long time because she's not willing to stop the offensive behavior. Should she return and continue to misbehave, then the parent can send her back to time-out, this time with a time limit.

Parents who get their children used to time-outs from the early years have a wonderful advantage over those who don't. Their youngsters usually don't have to spend so much energy testing limits because the parents have established a method of control that can be implemented fairly and consistently.

### *The "Logical Consequence"*

Often the best lesson a parent can teach a child is the *logical* consequence of the child's actions. If a youngster strays too far on his bicycle, doesn't it make more sense to take away his bike for a few days rather than to send him to bed early, tell him he can't watch television, or make him come in early from playing? Not only does this make sense, it makes sense to the child!

Many parents when asked will say that they definitely intend to let their youngsters suffer the consequences of their own misbehavior. But when it comes right down to it, many of these same parents balk at letting their youngsters suffer a natural consequence, usually because they want to spare their children disappointment or distress.

So kids blow their whole allowance on candy the day they receive it and their parents still give them more snack money later in the week. And parents sit up half the night helping their child complete a book report because they don't want him to get a lower grade, or they write out false excuses for tardiness that were just a matter of his not getting himself ready in time. Yes, the logical consequence in these situations wouldn't have been wonderful, but it probably would have provided the best lesson a child can learn—that he must take responsibility for his own actions.

Obviously there are some situations where the logical consequence would be outright dangerous. You wouldn't want your child to play in the street in order to get hit by a car and learn that such play was dangerous! Or to have a mouthful of cavities because he refused to brush and floss throughout childhood!

If done in a matter-of-fact fashion (rather than with vindictiveness or sarcasm), the logical consequence approach to discipline can eliminate potential power struggles. And kids seem to respond positively to the inherent logic and reasonableness that's involved.

### *Denying Privileges*

Sometimes there is no logical consequence for a child's actions, or none that would be reasonable to allow, and so a parent might decide to remove some privilege from the child. For example, if he runs around the supermarket and refuses to stay near the cart, the removed privilege could be anything from taking away television for the evening or setting an early bedtime to "grounding" or restricting him for a certain time period, depending upon the seriousness of the infraction.

Removal of a privilege is also useful when time-outs are not curtailing the troublesome behavior—if you've given Johnny four time-outs for standing on the furniture and he does it again. Some parents prefer removal of privileges to using time-outs, especially as their children get older.

Many parents err in viewing restrictions as all-or-nothing propositions. But there can be *degrees* of restriction lasting anywhere from a half a day to, in the event of a severe infraction, a week or two. You can ground a youngster to the front or back yard but he can still have his friends over. Or you can ground him to the house with no friends but he can still talk on the phone, have television, and so on. Or you can take away one or several privileges within the house or, in the most severe case, ground him to his room for several hours. In general it's best to restrict privileges more frequently but for short periods of time. Then you don't dig yourself into a hole with nothing left to take away!

If you use this type of discipline it's important to specify the length of time a child will be denied the privilege. If there's going to be a more general restriction, the youngster needs to be told what she has to do to have it lifted. For example, if you tell your child, "You're grounded until you improve your attitude!" you've really told her nothing that will help her move her behavior in a positive direction. Does this mean that one grumpy look at Mom will keep her grounded another week? Rather, "If you do your chores this week without making a big fuss, you may go to the party Saturday night and be off grounding" makes it clear what you're asking of her.

If privileges are going to be taken away for a week or more, you might want to give your child some options for earning back some or all of his privileges before the total restriction is over. If you destroy the child's hope, he might become bitter and uncooperative.

Sometimes, in anger, a parent will set a restriction that he later feels is too harsh. Or he realizes he's ended up punishing himself more than the child because he has to change his plans in order to carry out the discipline! For example, if you ground a youngster for two weeks when he's arranged to spend that second weekend with a friend while you are going on a trip you've planned, you've shot yourself in the foot unless you have a reliable overnight sitter! When this happens, tell your child you goofed. Let him know you're going to change the restriction to whatever you now think is reasonable. This approach lets your child know that you are a human being who makes mistakes and overreacts, but who also has the courage to admit it!

Using deprivation of privileges and restrictions in a reasonable way gives you the leverage you need as a parent to let your youngster know you are in control. Used unfairly or too severely, however, they're likely to increase your child's rebellion. If a youngster's attitude seems to worsen each day of restriction (either becoming angrier or more hopeless), it's possible you're being too severe or missing the mark on what's behind your child's behavior. Talk things over for a better mutual understanding, be open to possible compromise should your child suggest something reasonable, and don't hesitate to change your mind if you decide you've been unfair or too severe.

## Incentives

Many parents equate incentives with bribery and consequently don't want to use them. The truth is, however, that parents naturally tend to reward children for being cooperative. If your child is running amok in the aisles of the supermarket, it's highly unlikely that you're going to honor her request to stop for ice cream on the way home. If she has behaved cooperatively and then asks for ice cream, chances are you will either agree to get it or explain a good reason why you can't and promise to do it another day.

Now let's say a mother is standing at a checkout counter with a child who is screeching and wailing for a fifty-cent treat. If the mother gives in and buys the treat, she *is* bribing her youngster. The bribe is an act of desperation, not a positive use of incentives!

Or take the example of a mother who asks her son to get her a pair of scissors from the kitchen drawer and he refuses unless he can successfully negotiate a prize or treat for following his mother's request. Or the child who has been told she can earn a point on her reward chart for brushing her teeth but tries to raise the ante to two points. The parent who gives in to these kinds of situations is allowing herself to be bribed.

In other words, the potential for bribery is not in the incentive itself, but in the timing of the incentive and the type of behavior for which it is used. When you use an incentive correctly to motivate your child, you're reminding him *in advance* that you're going to allow some privilege or treat for certain behavior. And of course you're going to target certain specific behaviors and not give incentives for every time your child does something positive.

Another common objection to using incentives is that children need to develop an *internal* locus of control, and incentives represent control through an *external* source. This objection would certainly be valid if parents relied heavily on incentives and excluded other methods of teaching children self-control. Correctly used, incentives need to be targeted toward a child's specific behavior, not used as a motivation strategy for getting a youngster to do everything the parent wants her to do.

Correctly used, too, incentives can greatly speed behavior change in children. But the real goal is to get the child to *want* to behave correctly—not because of the incentive itself, but because the child feels better about herself when she's cooperative. Although children will begin to alter their problem behavior to get the reward or privilege, the incentive typically becomes of less consequence as the desired behavior change is obtained. The youngster feels the positive repercussions through the approval of her parents and through her increased self-esteem.

So let's say you've decided to use an incentive system with your child. Here are some tips to keep you from falling into the most common errors that can sabotage your success:

- **Give the reward as soon as possible after the child does what you've asked her to do.** The most common error parents make is to set a reward that takes too long for the child to earn (a trip to Disney Land, summer camp, a bike, or any other major purchase). What works, especially with young children, is a *daily* incentive combined, perhaps, with a *weekly* incentive. With this system, not only does the child get a chance each day to start over, but she also has the added bonus of looking forward to something special almost every day, should she do well.

- **Make it clear that the child is expected to do the behavior whether or not he earns the incentive.** The point is that the incentive is earned if the behavior is done *on time* and *without a hassle;* if the child is late or has a tantrum even though he does what was asked, he loses the incentive but still must perform the behavior. For example, if he's supposed to take a bath by eight o'clock and doesn't take it until nine (or has a tantrum before taking it!) he doesn't get the incentive. Or if he decides he doesn't want the incentive for some reason, he still must take the bath!

• **If you are using a chart system with points for daily activities, don't make it complicated.** Don't put too many items on the chart and don't get caught up in subtracting points, giving half points or figuring percentages. You don't want a chart that would take a CPA to figure out at the end of the week! You want your system to be simple enough for the child to understand.

• **Include the child in the process of developing the incentive system.** Even very young children need to be consulted about the incentive and, if a chart is made, the designing of the entire system. If the child is old enough to write, let her design the chart and present it to you for approval after you discuss the basic idea with her. Often kids have even better ideas than parents about solving these daily problems. Also, the more it's the "child's idea," the more likely she'll be to comply with it. Obviously you wouldn't accept a child's system unless it's reasonable ("I'll make my bed every day and you give me a hundred dollars every Friday, okay?"); remember that the system still needs to be parent-approved!

• **Don't put items on a chart that could occur once—or a hundred times—in one day.** Charts serve their function best when you are helping your child to remember to do daily or weekly requirements (such as chores). When you're trying to change problem behaviors that can recur many times in a day (fighting with siblings, interrupting other people when they talk, whining, not performing a request the first time it's asked, and other "attitudinal" problems), point out what you *want* your child to do instead (play cooperatively with siblings, allow other people to finish their sentences, and so on) and use an incentive system that gives the child the reward *immediately* after the desired behavior occurs. Coins, stickers, gold stars, and poker chips (which can't be swallowed!) are items that can be dispensed to reinforce a child right after the desired behavior occurs. These can be saved up for treats or privileges just like points on a chart.

• **Be generous.** Some parents are very stingy with incentives because they're afraid that they're going to foul everything up by giving too many points, chips, or other rewards. The reverse is actually true: The youngster needs to feel success, so you want to give her lots of opportunities to experience it. Better to have her earn ten chips a day to earn her evening reward than only three chips. After all, what you're looking for is the chance to reinforce desirable behavior!

• **Don't stop the system too soon.** Because incentive systems usually work fairly quickly to bring about behavior change, many parents stop them before the new behavior has really had a chance to take hold. Some parents continue charts but add new items (and larger incentives!) as the child grows older. Others simply decide to stop the whole system and come up with a new one if problems develop. If you're going to stop the system, present the idea to your child as a "graduation"—that he's now more grown up about doing whatever he's been working on, and in celebration of this fact you're now going to begin giving him an allowance (or raising the one he has), letting him have a slightly later bedtime, or giving some other privilege that reinforces the idea that he's reached a new level of maturity.

Remember that incentives should usually be privileges, not store-bought goodies. Tangible rewards should be used only when there is no other practical option. Common privileges include things like having a light on to read in bed for fifteen minutes after bedtime, having the radio (or cassette, stereo, or television) on for thirty minutes or until the child falls asleep, being able to play a video game for thirty minutes, an amount of television time for that evening, or having the dog sleep in the same room. Of course, kids are very unique in *their* definitions of what an incentive is. Some want a five-minute back rub from Mom, time on the family computer, or even being able to sit in Dad's favorite reclining chair after dinner! Where they're appropriate, be sure to incorporate their suggestions.

With very young children (and some older ones!) it can be very difficult to find an incentive that will hold their attention. This is a situation where a "goody bag" can help. A parent gets a number of all different kinds of *inexpensive* treats (dime-store fare), wraps them individually in tissue paper—so the child can't feel what they are—and places them in a bag or pillowcase. When the child earns a reward, she gets to reach into the goody bag and pull out a treat. Since all the treats are different, one that's not so exciting at the moment is not likely to ruin the child's motivation to work for the next one.

## Letting Kids Save Face

Because they are children, kids react in more childish ways when they are upset than the "mature adult" (theoretically!) does. After all, if a co-worker makes you angry, you're not likely to kick the wall, stick out your tongue at him, or make some obscene gesture at him—at least not in the presence of other people! Instead, you probably mentally rehearse some choice things you'd like to say but know better than to say out loud. You might tell a friend about your anger later, go play racquetball to work off some steam, or just go off privately and fume for awhile.

But kids are different. For example, let's take the youngster who gets sent to his room for time-out. He might give his parent a dirty look, stomp his feet, slink down the hallway rubbing his shoulder against the wall, mumble just loudly enough that his parent knows he's mumbling, slam the door, or do some other "immature" behavior (or a combination of several) to express his discontent.

Some parents will respond to such behaviors by yelling, increasing the amount of time the child must spend in time-out, making the child come back and walk down the hall properly, or lecturing him about the way he responds to discipline. What's happened is that the youngster has succeeded in pulling the grown-up's emotional chain and is basking in the pleasure of being able to get that grown-up superirritated! The point can also be reached where the cycle of anger escalates the punishment, piles up until it's ridiculous, and then the parent either has to back down and feel like a wimp or stick to it and feel like an ogre.

As another example, let's take a child who starts bouncing a basketball in the living room. His father says, "Allen, I don't want you bouncing balls in the living room. If you want to bouncc the ball, take it out on the patio." Now how many youngsters do you think would bounce that ball *one* more time on the way out to the patio? Probably most of them! But if you're the kind of parent who feels that your authority has been undermined by this one extra bounce and you become angry and more punitive as a result, you're probably the kind of parent who will invite power struggles with your child.

Certainly, not all face-saving behaviors should be ignored. Intense physical or verbal aggression calls for a parental reaction. A door slammed a little loudly to express anger can be let go; a door slammed so hard that pictures fall off the wall should not be ignored. The point is, whenever possible, it's generally more helpful to ignore a child's face-saving behavior than to respond to it.

Also, consider that a child needs *some* outlet for his anger at you, the powerful parent. If slamming a door gives him a little release, why not? He's probably showing some self-control since he might really like to scream and throw things!

So ignore the things you can ignore when you are disciplining your child. Your power isn't based on having the "last word."

## Nag Proofing Yourself

Most adults agree that being nagged is very aggravating and makes them feel rebellious even, and especially, if the person doing the nagging is perfectly "right." Yet parents continue to nag their kids to do things and then wonder "Why do I always have to become a nag to get this kid to do something?"

A way out of this problem is to set *time limits* for the things you want your child to do. This doesn't necessarily mean clock-time; it could mean before school, after school but before going outside or using the phone, before a certain television program, before dinner, before bedtime, and so on. The point is that once you have established that a chore is to be done by a certain time, you automatically eliminate the need to nag your child about that chore until that time limit arrives. When it does, you can insist that "all fun things stop" until the chore is done.

For example, rather than bugging your child every fifteen minutes about whether or not she's gotten her homework done, talk with her and establish a time when homework must be finished. If the time limit is seven o'clock and her homework isn't finished (or even started!) by seven, all other activities stop—for the child—until that homework gets completed. Whether she misses ten minutes of her favorite television show or the entire evening of television depends upon when she gets that homework done!

## Being Human!

Why is being human listed as a parental skill? Simply to point out that many parents have an unrealistic view about being a "good parent." They set up an expectation that goes something like this: "I shall always be consistent, fair, calm, reasonable, instantly forgiving, available, cheerful, understanding, positive, and totally loving. Above all, I will never 'lose it' with my child."

While these are noble intentions, an important critical ingredient has been left out: being human! It would be totally impossible for anyone but a robot (with a perfect programmer) to live up to that kind of self-expectation. While it's fine to implement "parenting skills" and to be attuned to the impact of your behavior on your child, remember that the most important thing you want to do with your youngster is to *connect* with her *emotionally.* Except in the extreme situation where physical or verbal abuse is involved, it sometimes helps a lot to "lose it" and show your child that you are indeed a human being with feelings and vulnerabilities. The normally calm, reasonable parent who suddenly yells, bursts into tears, behaves inconsistently out of exasperation, or who goes to her room and isolates herself for a while is making a statement that, *if it's not overused,* can have a powerfully positive effect on a child. He knows he has a parent who's *real* and not cut out of some mold designed by a parenting "expert."

## A REMINDER

Before we get into the nitty-gritty of how to handle specific "hot spot" situations, it's important for you to realize that what works with one child might not work with another. Also, your own temperament and personality as a parent will influence your comfort level and success with any particular "technique." Your talking and listening skills will be important, as well as your ability to give your youngster sincere praise. Sometimes that "hot seat" sensation will disappear simply by staying calm and listening to your child. And in some cases, realizing that your "hot seat" sensation is more *your* problem than your child's is the key. It may be best to do nothing specific with your youngster and instead have a good talk with yourself to calm things down!

Above all, realize that you won't always have "the answer" (whatever that is), and you'll certainly goof on occasion. Know that it's totally normal to feel self-conscious about your child's behavior when you're in front of other people. But think this through: There will always be cranky people who judge others. There are people who just don't care much for children, period. And there are folks who've never had kids but have all kinds of opinions about child raising without the benefit of any practical, in-the-trenches experience.

It comes down to the realization that not everybody is going to like everything you do, and your parenting strategies are no exception. You just have to get clear about your intentions, do the best you can, and ignore any little barbs of criticism that might come your way.

Rest assured that these not-so-wonderful little moments with your child are as natural as rain. Kids of all ages will suddenly say or do things that are horrid, outrageous, or very difficult to tolerate. This doesn't mean you've done anything wrong or that your child is psychologically disturbed! Remember, what matters is that your heart is in the right place, that you keep on keeping on, and that you *emotionally* connect with your child.

## WHAT'S COMING UP?

In the chapters that follow, you'll find some ideas about what to do when your child backs you into a corner, freaks you out, makes you feel like a fool or momentarily causes you to consider strangling her. Through the use of classic vignettes you'll be given some thoughts about what could be going on with your child in these situations, as well as some practical strategies for handling those frustrating (and maddening) quandaries that come with being a parent. Whether the situation occurs in your favorite restaurant or in your own living room, you'll be given ideas to use on the spot when the situation occurs, as well as some thoughts about how to keep such a problem from starting or recurring.

Ultimately, this book will help you to reduce those moments when you are utterly confused and bewildered as a parent. It's my hope that, through reading it, you'll find yourself in the "hot seat" less often—but that when you're there, you'll know what to do!

# CHAPTER 2

## *The Daily Routine*

One of the good things about having a routine every day is that you can put at least one part of your life on automatic pilot. You don't have to think about putting on your clothes in the morning, making the coffee, brushing your teeth, closing the drapes before bedtime, or locking the door before you leave home. You don't give these things much thought—you just do them, probably in a timely manner. Routines help to move the day forward.

As a parent, you know it's also good for your child to have a predictable routine. Inconsistency will often inspire power struggles and arguments. Kids are less anxious when they experience some structure in their lives. They take comfort from knowing they do the same thing at roughly the same time every day.

Consequently, most parents get extremely frustrated and perplexed when a child refuses to cooperate with what should be a routine daily activity like getting dressed, eating meals, taking care of hygiene, and going to bed at night. Yet kids are notorious for making these events (that should be so simple) into a battleground. *Why?*

First, any child—even the most well-behaved—will test limits by purposely breaking a rule. It's a kid's way of finding out if a parent really means business. If the parent follows through with discipline, the child knows he can trust that parent to react the same way if he fouls up again. The child also finds out that a parent cares enough to notice his behavior and to take the necessary time to react appropriately. This reassures him that he really can't get out of control and is, therefore, safe—even from his own impulses.

Second, parents sometimes unintentionally encourage their kids to rebel against rules and routines by setting too many rules or by being too rigid and inflexible. Yes, consistency is important, but there are also times when common sense tells a parent to ease up a little. Parents are supposed to be nurturers, not drill sergeants. Still, it's hard to know when it's time to let up.

Many parents worry that if they relax a rule *one* time, there'll be a fight the *next* time. Whether this happens will often depend on whether or not the routine has become a battleground. If it's been causing a hassle around the house, it's probably better for a parent to stick to her guns and enforce the rule. Or, if the child has been testing limits on most house rules, this is not likely to be the best time to ease up on consistency. On the other hand, if the child has been following the routine fairly regularly but has suddenly expressed a desire to do things a new way, letting up might be a good way to handle the situation. Kids are great at figuring out when a parent really means "Just this once, honey" and when those words only signal that a parent is an easy mark for manipulation.

Now let's look at some of the common hassles about these supposedly ordinary routine events that can really put a parent on the spot.

### The Morning Grump

**You need to get to work a little early this morning and have no time to spare. You stop into eight-year-old Jeremy's room to wake him up, kiss his forehead, and tell him, "Wake up, sweetie, time to get going." Although you explain that you need to get an early start on a very busy day, Jeremy responds like the mad thrasher, pulls the covers over his head, and won't budge. There's just no time for persuading, reasoning, threatening, or negotiating; you've *got* to get this kid up!**

Summon your best no-nonsense voice, pull the covers off the grumpy body, and tell him, "Get up, Jeremy, right now. There's no time to fool around." The point is to mean it—with your words, your tone of voice, and your body language. If you sound apologetic or wishy-washy, your youngster's emotional antennae will pick this up and he'll be more likely to continue stalling.

However, don't expect him to be pleasant about getting up. He'll probably be anything but friendly. In fact, if looks could kill, you'd be long gone. Just ignore this negativity and matter-of-factly point out that his clothes are laid out and waiting for a body to fill them.

But what if he flatly refuses to get up? Terrible as you might feel, you really have little choice but to physically get him out of bed. This demonstrates that there are some situations that just aren't negotiable.

To avoid a repeat of this problem, catch Jeremy later when he's in a better mood. Explain that you're not going to bother getting him up anymore since it seems to make him so angry. Tell him you're buying him an alarm clock and that he'll be responsible for getting himself up.

"Oh brother," you're thinking. "This will never work! My kid will sleep right on through any alarm." Well, not if you teach him not to. But how?

Of course there is a trick. The key is to get a very loud alarm, one that doesn't stop ringing until it's turned off. Place the clock across the room from your child's bed, forcing him to get out of bed to turn it off. Reassure him that after he's accustomed to getting up to the alarm, he can move it closer to his bed—as long as he continues getting up and doesn't put it on perpetual snooze.

A word of caution. Many children will continue sleeping right on through even the most deafening of alarms until they learn the habit of waking up to it. In such a situation, you can call out to your child, or bang on his door, to get him to wake up. But don't make the mistake of turning off the alarm. Insist that he get out of bed to turn it off himself. This tactic will allow you to create a habit in your child rather than in yourself.

For the preschooler who's typically too young for an alarm, try handling grumpiness by saying something like "Honey, you seem to be having a hard time this morning. Would a hug help?" If your youngster doesn't respond to this, ignoring his cranky behavior and remaining cheerful yourself will keep you from reinforcing his negative behavior.

If you start taking your youngster's wake-up grumpiness personally, remember that many well-adjusted adults are simply not morning people either. You probably know of someone (maybe even you!) who doesn't become civil until after that first cup of coffee.

To prevent morning grumpiness from becoming a problem in the first place, be sure that your child is getting enough rest. Remember, kids have biorhythms too. Also, your youngster may best be roused from her sleepy state with a little morning cuddling, though some children dislike to be touched or spoken to any more than is absolutely necessary. Some youngsters like to have their environment calm and quiet in the morning; others prefer the dog to be running around the room and their favorite music tape to be blasting away (within reason, please!) in the background.

The point is, respect your child's own unique style of making the transition from sleep to activity. Let her get up earlier if she likes to be a slow mover; let her sleep a little later if she wants to stay in bed until the last possible moment and then flip into high gear.

### The Home Wrecker

**Two-year-old Amy has spent most of the morning running from one nontouchable object to another. You realize you've been screaming *no* every five minutes, Amy is looking stressed-out, and you feel you're turning into a megamonster. Suddenly, she's climbing up on a chair to reach the picture frame with your wedding photo, which you carefully placed out of her reach. How do you stop her without squelching her natural inquisitive spirit?**

Quickly remove her from the chair and firmly tell her, "No no, Amy, you mustn't touch that. It's not a toy." Then distract her by removing her to another location and giving her something she *can* play with. If she gets up and heads back to the scene of the crime, pick her up and put her back where you want her, saying something like "No, Amy, I told you, you can't touch the things on the tables and shelves unless I tell you it's okay. Now I want you to sit right here." If she continues to test you, you could give her a time-out in a chair or put her in a place where she can't escape, such as a playpen or even her crib.

If this tactic works most of the time, you're home free. But there are some children who are highly active, highly persistent, and/or highly oppositional. They'll repeatedly try to touch everything in sight, including pulling pans out of your kitchen cabinets and climbing like monkeys to reach the supposedly unreachable. If your child has this kind of temperament, you'd be constantly saying no to her, leaving both of you feeling consistently upset. Especially for very young children, it's usually best to minimize temptation. Get cabinet guards and put breakable or fragile objects in a place where your youngster can't get to them until she's older and more able to understand your requests about not touching.

Most important, take a good look at your furnishings and then at your expectations. Even with a child who's not highly active, is your house a comfortable place not just for you, but also for your child? Is there a place where your child can play in the living area? Are there so many knickknacks within your child's reach that you mentally wince every time she walks by?

It's not necessary to turn your house into one big playroom, but it makes good sense to have a minimum of "no-touch" items in rooms where your child will be spending a lot of time. If you worry that your child won't learn self-control if you accommodate the house to her needs, rest assured that you'll still have plenty of opportunities to say no to her even in a childproof house. You'll have enough of a struggle being consistent about teaching Miss Curious not to touch dangerous objects (electric wires and outlets) or items that can't be put away (television controls, lamps). The point is that you don't want to have to engage in an overabundance of power plays.

## The Picky Eater

**It's thirty minutes after dinner is over, but you're still sitting at the table with four-year-old Samantha. She sits with a skeptical frown as you doggedly continue making choochoo trains out of peas, trying to chug each one past her reluctant lips. You're sick of this little game, your other kids need you, and you've got to do the laundry if you want clean underwear for work tomorrow. You're getting frantic, but your kid's got to eat!**

Tell Samantha dinner's over, remove her food, and spare yourself this agony. It won't work. Sure, you might cram a few more bites of food into her—if you're willing to sit there long enough—but that's not teaching her to eat appropriately. In fact, what you're teaching her is that by not eating, or being balky and finicky, she can capture the total attention of an adult. After all, she's successfully keeping you from having time with your spouse, your other kids, or even yourself. What power!

Begin a new strategy immediately. At mealtime, make the food available to everyone. After a suitable length of time, remove whatever hasn't been eaten. Whether Samantha has eaten nothing, taken two bites, or cleaned her plate, remain matter-of-fact. If she's eaten an appropriate amount, let her know she can have her usual snacks before the next meal, or before bed. If she hasn't eaten enough, tell her there will be no more food until the next meal. It's that simple!

Of course, she might protest mightily a few times. She's testing you. But if you stick to your guns, she'll learn that you really mean what you say—not only in this situation, but in others as well. You make yourself clear, you remain consistent, and, presto—her constant testing of your rules becomes a thing of the past.

Now you might think this idea is great for breakfast and lunch, but you could be having qualms about putting this plan into effect at dinner. "What? Send my poor child to bed with no food?" you're wondering.

You know rationally that your child won't starve to death by missing a meal, even several meals. But if you're going to lie awake because you can't bear the thought of your child's not having anything to eat before bedtime, you can let her have some food that is okay but unexciting to her. Not cake, her favorite sandwich, or her special Disneyland cereal, but not something she hates either. Just something ho-hum.

To prevent power struggles over eating from getting started in the first place, don't make an issue of how much or how little your child eats. Give small portions and allow your youngster to ask for seconds rather than worrying about wasting food. Set reasonable limits on portions so your child doesn't wind up eating only two or three specific foods (consuming five bowls of her favorite cereal). Try to make sure that *something* your child likes to eat is on every menu. If you're pretty sure she's not too thrilled about your main selection—and if it's not too inconvenient—offer your youngster a choice between two foods. But this certainly doesn't mean that you should turn yourself into a short-order cook to please your child's every whim!

Also, remember to ask yourself if your child is getting enough one-on-one attention. You'll want her to know that she can have times of undivided parental attention without having to resort to creating a power struggle over eating.

### "Give Me Back My Diaper!"

**You've just introduced three-year-old Mike to his new potty seat, shown him his new superhero underpants, and explained the glories of being a "big boy" and using the toilet like Daddy. To your delight, he makes a BM in the toilet a couple of times. But then, to your horror, he starts screaming, "I want my diaper back!"**

Let him have his diaper back! It's not worth developing a power struggle, which is exactly what will happen if you become insistent on toilet training him against his will.

Many children, especially boys, are just not physiologically ready to be toilet trained until about age three because they haven't developed adequate bladder or sphincter control. Even if your child is physically ready, it's still a good idea to wait until he becomes more cooperative before you begin a campaign for him to use the potty. But why?

Remember the old saying about the "terrible two's"? That's the developmental stage, usually around age two, when kids begin to exert their independence, usually by a liberal use of the word "no." Many youngsters at this age become very negative, challenging every request their parents make of them. For the child's emotional development to progress without undue glitches, a parent's job at this point is to give the child *some* choice without allowing the child to dictate the rules. For example, Mom might give her two-year-old a choice between cereal and pancakes for breakfast, but she would not offer the contents of the entire pantry and refrigerator just to suit her child's capricious desires.

Handled successfully, a child will move out of the negativism of the "terrible two's" and become reasonably cooperative. Handled unsuccessfully, he's likely to continue to invite a parent into numerous power struggles. It just makes common sense, then, to wait until your child has moved out of an uncooperative state of mind before you attempt toilet training. Besides, a power struggle over withholding BMs and soiling underpants is not much fun.

Realize, too, that your child might have his own reasons for not wanting to "grow up and be a big boy" right at the moment you want to throw away the diapers. After all, many children in the two- to three-year-old range are struggling with a new baby brother or sister. And since they're already insecure about their place in their parents' affection due to the new arrival, the last thing they want to do is to give up being a baby themselves.

When you think your child is ready for the potty—when he indicates he wants to try it out and he's able to stay dry at least two hours—encourage him to use it. If he's interested one day and not the next, go with his mood for a time. If he's totally uninterested and has to be coerced, it's not a good time to start potty training.

When your youngster climbs on the potty, tell him to go to the bathroom. If nothing comes out of him after a minute or so, let him know he doesn't need to go just yet. Let him get off the toilet with the reminder that he can try again whenever he feels ready. This matter-of-fact handling of the bathroom business keeps the whole process from becoming a battle of wills.

## The Bed Wetter

**Six-year-old Danny's bed-wetting is driving you nuts. And now you've planned a family camping trip that's a month away. Thinking about a wet sleeping bag strengthens your resolve to do something now, but what?**

While this might *feel* like a real "hot seat" situation, you're only torturing yourself if you expect to come up with an instant solution. Not only is Danny's bed-wetting not under your control, it's probably not under his either. Of course you'll want to work with your son on this problem, but try to eliminate your feelings of urgency. They will probably get transmitted to him and only make matters worse.

There are several approaches that might eventually solve this problem (but probably not for the camping trip in one month!). First, however, it's important to understand a bit about children's bed-wetting.

A common mistake is to assume that the cause of your child's bed-wetting is "emotional." If a youngster has had a long period of *not* wetting the bed (several months) and then begins to wet consistently again, he could have a urinary tract infection. Once your doctor has ruled this out, you could then look to a possible emotional cause (regression due to a new baby in the family; a traumatic event; something that's bothering him about himself, school, or his family; sexual or physical abuse, etc.). If this is the case, you would obviously want to address the underlying emotional issue as well as incorporate some of the suggestions for management of the bed-wetting that are described in the next few pages.

If you have a youngster who has *never* been consistently dry at night, there could be other causes of his wetting, *not* emotional in origin. In fact, this type of bed-wetting is often hereditary. One cause could be a physical problem with the bladder or kidneys; consequently, the child should always be checked by a physician to rule this out.

If no physical disorder can be found, one cause for a child's wetting might be that he's a very heavy sleeper and almost impossible to wake up during the night. The youngster sleeps so deeply that the signals sent by his full bladder don't trigger his brain to wake up, as they do in a child who has a lighter sleep pattern. In fact, it does little good for a parent to make a half-asleep child get up in the night to go to the bathroom. This tactic, unfortunately, only *reinforces* his urinating while he's asleep, and results in training the parent rather than the child! So what are your options?

First, many pediatricians will prescribe a medication that might help a youngster stay dry at night. After several months on the medicine, many children are able to stop taking it without resuming their bed-wetting. It's as if their brains have been "retrained" to pay attention to bladder cues. Medications, of course, can have side effects, so your doctor might not want to recommend medicine for your child's particular situation.

Second, you might opt to instruct your youngster in bladder-training exercises. This regimen involves training a child to increase the volume of urine in his bladder without urinating, and then learning to interrupt his urine stream in the process of voiding. These exercises are designed to increase bladder tone, and your doctor would be the best person to instruct you in the specifics of this method.

Third, you might want to purchase an alarm device specifically made for bed wetters. Basically, these systems involve the child's wearing a simple device on or near his undergarments that signals an alarm or buzzer when the device becomes slightly wet. The child learns to awaken to the alarm when he first begins to urinate, and can proceed to the bathroom to void the contents of his bladder. There are several types of alarm devices available, and they vary in price.

Fourth, if your child is *highly motivated* to stop wetting the bed, he might be agreeable to setting his alarm and getting up at night (waking fully) to go to the bathroom. A typical plan might be to set his alarm at midnight or 1:00 A.M. If he is dry when he wakes up, he would reset his alarm to 2:00 A.M. the next night. Every night that he's dry, he'd increase the hour for the alarm. At some point, of course, he would find a wet bed, in which case he'd know that he would have to go back to setting his alarm a little earlier. By pinpointing the time of wetting, he can control it by getting up beforehand to urinate.

Whether you think your youngster is bed-wetting because of physical or emotional causes, let him take as much responsibility for the consequences as his age will allow. For instance, put a stack of clean towels and pajamas in his bedroom; if he awakens in the night after wetting, he can change his nightclothes and put a towel over his wet sheet until morning (rather than waking you up to do it). In the morning, even a young child can strip his bed and put the sheets in a plastic bag provided for him. The older youngster can be taught to launder his own bed linens and to make his bed with clean sheets.

There are many advantages to having a child take this responsibility upon himself. Obviously, one is that the parent doesn't have to do all the work. But there are other positive reasons. First, to the extent that a child might be consciously or subconsciously using bed-wetting to punish a parent, this approach eliminates that opportunity, and he may become more motivated to stop wetting when he has to take care of the wet clothes and linens himself. Second, and perhaps most important, the more the child assumes responsibility for the consequences of his wetting, the less needs to be said about it in the family. The child gets the healthy message that he'll quit wetting one day when he's ready, and in the meantime, it's "no big deal." In fact, this casual, matter-of-fact approach is best, whether or not the bed-wetting is under the child's control, since it minimizes the potential self-esteem problems that can occur in youngsters who wet the bed.

## "I'll Make My BM Anywhere but in the Toilet!"

**Five-year-old Nathan continues to make his BMs in his pants. You've decided you're going to remain calm because, after all, the poor kid just gets involved in playing and can't quite make it to the toilet in time; he'd certainly control it if he could. Then one day you spot him standing behind your ficus tree, nonchalantly soiling in his pants!**

Even though the light has dawned and you realize your child is *choosing* to soil his pants, state as matter-of-factly as you can something like "Nathan, you need to make your BMs in the toilet. Go into the bathroom and finish up there. And by the way, you'll need to start cleaning yourself up when your bottom is dirty, and you'll also need to start washing out your own underwear. I'll put out the wipes for your bottom, and you can use the soap to scrub your pants. If there's BM in your pants, dump it into the toilet and flush it away before you wash the stains out of your underwear."

Nathan, of course, will probably not like this new chore you've assigned him. Just let him handle it, providing only emotional support and strategic suggestions, no matter how much he might protest. If he gets himself messier trying to clean up, tell him to take a bubble bath and soap himself off.

Sound cruel? No, it's just the logical consequence a person faces when he chooses to soil his pants rather than use the toilet. What you're doing with this strategy is making sure your child gets *zero* extra attention for this behavior.

In addition to assigning the negative consequence of cleaning up the mess, you could also give your youngster some positive incentive for depositing his BMs in the toilet. But this can get tricky. For instance, if you decide to give him a small prize or token for making his BM in the toilet, he might start running to the john every few minutes and making minuscule deposits just to get more goodies. Even worse, lucky you has to bird-dog what is and isn't left in the toilet. All of this only adds to the attention and fuss about what should be an easy, normal, personal bodily function. So to get around this problem, reward clean underpants at the end of the day rather than the contents of the potty.

It's always wise to check with your pediatrician or pediatric gastroenterologist about the medical aspects of your child's soiling, as there can be physical causes for this problem. Even if no physical cause can be found, most kids who choose to continue soiling when they are capable of using the toilet will withhold their BMs as long as they can. Many doctors recommend a high-fiber diet with plenty of fluids to ensure that the child's bowels don't become impacted in the intestines, sometimes prescribing medicine to keep the stool soft if dietary measures don't solve the difficulty.

If the soiling problem doesn't improve, you'll probably need to consult a mental health professional to help figure out why your child is in such a power struggle. Because that's what soiling (without a physical cause) in a school-age child is—a giant power struggle with some adult.

To help prevent such power struggles from forming in the first place, strike a balance between the extremes of overcontrol and permissiveness. If a child is squelched by a parent who absolutely insists on the parent's wishes in spite of the child's preferences, he's likely to become overly compliant or overly rebellious, depending on his basic temperament. On the other hand, if he's given carte blanche to be a total free spirit, he's likely to become egocentric and demanding.

The middle ground for this age-old dilemma is to give a child two, perhaps three, options *if it's reasonable to do so.* (If it's twenty degrees outside, you don't give your child a choice about whether or not to wear a coat when he goes outside! But if he's resisting wearing an outfit you've picked out for him, you might give him one other suitable option.)

If a child develops a soiling problem, it *may* mean that he's been overcontrolled. From the child's viewpoint, he could be saying, "You can make me do lots of things, but you can't control how or when I make my BMs!" If you're setting too many rules or insisting on absolute obedience without ever letting your child express disagreement, you'll need to lighten up.

### "I Hate Baths!"

**Eight-year-old Mark has just returned from baseball practice utterly filthy and is flatly refusing to take a bath. You're at your wit's end arguing with him and are wondering if you're going to have to forcibly drag him into the tub!**

First, you might ask yourself if you need to rethink the dirt issue. There's a difference between the child who refuses to bathe most of the time and the youngster who sometimes skips a bath because of exhaustion or a hectic schedule. Sometimes giving your child a "compassionate break" from a routine pays you back tenfold in goodwill and future cooperation.

If you decide you must force the issue, cut the argument short with "Mark, I'm giving you three minutes to get into that tub. If you don't make it, you'll have a negative consequence you're not going to like." You don't have to know what the consequence will be at that moment. Give yourself time to think it through. If your child demands to know what the penalty will be, repeat that his concern should be getting to the tub; you'll tell him about the consequence later.

Should he still refuse, you can send him to his room until he complies, or to bed if it's that time of night. If he goes to sleep dirty, you could let him know he'll be getting up fifteen minutes early in the morning to bathe. And if his sheets end up being dirty, let him wash them!

If you and your child are battling over bathing, brushing teeth, or some other hygiene issue, the solution will not be found in nagging, threatening, or lecturing. Instead, set a time limit for him to complete the behavior (before he leaves for school, before he watches his morning cartoons, before supper, by eight o'clock, etc.). If he doesn't accomplish the task by the time limit, everything fun stops until he complies.

For example, if he's supposed to bathe before eight o'clock at night and doesn't, no television, video games, telephone, snacking, playing, etc. until the bath is taken. If she's supposed to brush her teeth before she leaves for school and doesn't, her first task when she comes home will be to brush those teeth—even before her after-school snack. In other words, set a time limit so you won't have to nag; then enforce the "everything stops until it's done" philosophy so your youngster doesn't learn that these necessary grooming matters can be avoided.

If you want to speed up the process of getting your youngster to cooperate, you could add an incentive system. By your temporarily allowing him to earn a privilege or reward for bathing on time until the new habit is formed, he's likely to be more enthusiastic right from the beginning.

### "I DON'T WANT TO GET UP!"

**You wake up seven-year-old Susan, leave her with all her clothes set out on the bed, and hurry to the kitchen to fix breakfast. Twenty minutes later she still hasn't appeared to eat, and you decide to check up on her. You walk into her room to find her sitting nude on the bed, wearing only one sock!**

Be positive. Tell her, "Hey, you got your sock on! Better hurry, though; your car pool will be here in fifteen minutes!" Then leave the room, letting Susan have the responsibility for finishing getting dressed.

If the weather outside is warm, you're lucky enough to get to use logical consequences. If Susan isn't dressed by the time the car pool arrives, simply take all the items that aren't properly attached to her (except basic covering for decency), put them in a bag, and let her finish dressing in the car or in the school rest room. Yes, she'll be shocked. But it's very likely she won't dawdle quite so much in the future. The message is clear: If she wastes time getting ready for a deadline, she'll just have to dress in less convenient circumstances.

If it's cold outside, you'll need to dress your child in warm clothing before sending her out into the elements. Even then, you can send the "extras" in a bag (a brush or comb, belt, barrettes, ribbons, and jewelry) rather than getting her picture-perfect.

Many parents yell, threaten, or often take over some or all of the dressing when their kids aren't properly dressed. Barrettes are quickly jammed into hunks of hair, arms are shoved into tops, and feet are scrunched hastily into shoes—usually with the child scowling, pouting, or even crying. Unfortunately, what the child usually learns from all this negative activity is that, when push comes to shove, a parent will take over and make sure the child gets dressed. By placing the responsibility squarely on the child, sticking to the normal schedule (rather than waiting for the youngster to finish dressing), and remaining calm, a parent teaches an effective lesson without developing a power struggle.

While it might be necessary to go ahead and dress your child in a situation where there is *no* choice (you have to get to work and are the only source of transportation), consider first whether there might be another option. For instance, you might let your child dress herself and be late to school (though not habitually!). Unless you have a youngster who hates school and couldn't care less about the teacher admonishing her for being late, one remark from that teacher about being tardy might totally eliminate the dawdling problem.

Since prevention is the best cure, you might consider changing your child's morning environment so that she's more likely to get dressed on time. For example, if she's distractible and is used to getting dressed in a room with a sibling, a turned-on television, and/or a dog running around, eliminate the sources of distraction. Have your kid get dressed in a separate room, ban pets from the dressing arena, and make the favorite morning television show something that is turned on only *after* she's dressed (if at all). Try setting a timer where your child can see the time elapsing to help her stay on track. It also helps to select clothing and set it out the night before so your child doesn't get bogged down in making choices the next morning.

## "I Don't Want to Clean Up!"

**Story time is over and it's time for four-year-old Bobby to go to bed. You walk him to his room to tuck him in for the night, only to discover the floor of his room strewn with crayons, miniature cars, building blocks, and an assortment of stuffed animals. Even worse, his bed is covered with seashells collected from last weekend's trip to the beach.**

He's still young, so make cleanup a team project. Tell him, "Uh-oh, Bobby! We've got a problem! All these toys need to be put back in their places. Come on, you gather up the animals and put them on the shelf; I'll start with the shells. Let's see how quickly we can get this room back in shape!"

Ideally, you want your child to form the habit of cleaning up his toys after he's finished playing with them. But a young child can be overwhelmed if the job is too large. Better to give him some simple instructions about where to start the cleanup process and help him along by pitching in to get things straight.

If the same problem keeps occurring, give your youngster a time limit for picking up his toys. For an older child, this could be a specific time on the clock. For the younger child who can't tell time, give him appropriate time limits such as before supper, before evening television, before bath time, before the bedtime story, etc. If the toys aren't picked up by the time limit, then all else stops until they are! This tactic keeps you from having to nag your child all day long about remembering something he's supposed to do, but it provides a definite consequence for him if he doesn't follow up by the time limit.

### "I Can't Sleep!"

**You've been waiting all evening for that delicious time alone with your spouse. The candles are waiting, the CD is geared up for Rachmaninoff, and your new teddy hangs invitingly on the bathroom doorknob. Just as you shut the bedroom door, there comes seven-year-old Josh down the hall, asking for his third drink of water!**

Realize that your momentary urge to throttle your child for ruining your sex life is totally normal. Then move on to the problem at hand.

What you want to do is to get your child back in bed with matter-of-fact efficiency and without reinforcing his attention-seeking behavior. That means no more rituals, no more drinks, no more songs and kisses, no more explaining.

Tell him something short and to the point like "It's time for bed" or "I want you to stay in bed until morning." Calmly lead him or pick him up and carry him back to his room, put him in bed, cover him up without ceremony, turn out the light, and leave the room.

If your youngster again gets out of bed—and he probably will the first few times you try this—repeat the same procedure. What you're doing is showing him you mean what you say. Be prepared to repeat this behavior many times for a few nights. So long as you remain consistent and do not give your child extra attention, he will eventually get the point and quit testing you.

You might wonder why you shouldn't simply reason with your child about why he should go to bed: "You have school. It's hard for you to get up in the morning," for example. You might be tempted to get your reluctant youngster back into bed by pacifying him with another drink, another kiss, another story, another back rub, another song, another something. You might also want to carry the youngster back to his bed and retuck him in, repeating all or part of the usual bedtime ritual.

The problem is, all of this talking, reasoning, and kissing only reinforces a child's *not* going to bed. In fact, the youngster has mastered the art of getting at least one of his parents, if not two, to give him total attention. The whole world at home is revolving around one little person.

But in exasperation, you will probably only end up angry and yelling at the child to stay in bed. Whether yelling, threatening to spank, or just getting red-faced, your child knows he's gotten to you. Though negative, your behavior is still reinforcing to him.

If your child has made a habit of delaying bedtime and you're gearing up to change this situation, it might shorten the process if you offer him some incentive for staying in his bed. He could cash in the next day by receiving the treat or privilege he earned by going to bed promptly and without fuss. Whenever he gets up again, you'd still react with the matter-of-fact approach just described.

You might be tempted to try to help your child stay in bed by lying down with him until he falls asleep. Typically, this tactic will work well the first few times you use it and your child will fall asleep within minutes. There's just one problem: The length of time you must remain will soon begin to increase as your child quickly realizes he's in control. Parents have been known to stay in the child's room for an hour or two, sometimes even giving up and falling asleep with the child for the night.

There are certainly occasions when your child is upset about something and you might decide that you want to lie down with him for a little while. There's nothing wrong with this as long as you keep the time short. Five or ten minutes is appropriate; when it stretches beyond that, you're losing a power struggle.

Be prepared to spend a few evenings consistently and matter-of-factly following through with putting your child back to bed each and every time he reappears. You'll be ensuring your right to have some free time from dealing with children as well as preserving your sanity—and your sex life.

### The Late Diner

**Nine-year-old Sally is playing with the neighbors' kids in the backyard when it's time for dinner. You call to her to come in and eat, but she remains out in the yard as long as she possibly can. You realize that this has become a pattern, you've clearly warned her of the consequences, and now you've decided you've had it!**

Don't hold dinner for Sally! Go ahead and let everyone begin eating. Allow the logical consequences to take place, which might be that Sally's food will be cold or that all the drumsticks she loves so much already will have been eaten! In fact, if all the food is gone, she'll just have to fix herself something generic and unexciting, like a bowl of cereal or soup.

What usually happens, however, is that a parent will give a child several calls (each one louder in volume!) to a meal until that parent is furious about being made to wait. Everyone who is ready for the meal is irritated at the inconvenience, not to mention the rapidly cooling food on their plates. The meal starts off on a bad note, nobody feels much like conversation, and everyone's digestion is at risk. As for the child, she learns not to listen to a first (or fourth) call for meals, that the grown-ups will wait for her, and that she's the center of attention.

By experiencing the logical consequences of her behavior, Sally will quickly learn that she must listen to a call to come for dinner and not dawdle about getting into the house. Nobody is inconvenienced, nobody becomes upset (except maybe Sally, when she finds her favorite goodies are gone!), and Sally learns that she is not in control of the household. Of course, it's important to let her know ahead of time how long she can play before dinner and to give her a ten-minute warning before mealtime begins.

### The Kid Who Can't Shift Gears

**Six-year-old Jennifer is playing house in the living area and has made a tent out of the dining room table. Your dinner company is arriving soon, and you pleasantly ask Jennifer to remove the tent and her dolls to her room and to get dressed for company. Much to your amazement, she throws a tantrum and refuses to budge from under the table!**

Retrieve Jennifer from under the table (fortunately, adults are usually bigger and stronger than young kids!) and take her to her room. Tell her you're sorry you forgot to warn her earlier about cleaning up and getting dressed, and offer to help her get started. If she continues her tantrum, leave her in her room with instructions to call you if she wants help when she's ready to get dressed. Pick up the tent and the toys yourself, and chalk the whole thing up to poor timing and classic childhood behavior.

While some kids are very flexible and have no problems with changing from one activity to another, many youngsters are very resistant to any change in their schedule—even if it's a positive change. In fact, research has shown that the ease with which a child adapts to change is a matter of temperament. In other words, babies are different in this respect, right from birth.

If your child is the type who balks with change, it will help keep confrontations to a minimum if you give her a friendly warning before the time comes for a change in activity. For example, if she's watching television before bed, you might let her know when the show begins that she'll need to stop watching at the end of it, and then give her a five-minute warning again before the show is over. If she's going to have to stop watching television in the middle of a program, let her know this in advance. If you know from past experience that she'll still get upset if she can't see the entire program, tell her you will not allow her to start the program since it's so hard for her to be interrupted.

This same tactic can be applied any time you are going to vary your child's daily routine or to take her away from some pleasant activity. For example, if she's playing at a friend's house, give her a couple of warnings before it's actually time to leave.

When you've forgotten to give a warning, or if circumstances are such that you have no time to give one, understand that your child's balkiness is caused by the disruption in routine or expectation rather than by her being out to make your life miserable. When she's quieted down and becomes cooperative again, explain to her that you know it's difficult for her to change her plans and that you'll try to give her advance notice whenever possible. And let her know that this problem is something you must work on together because warnings aren't always practical. In other words, teach your child about her own temperament so that as she grows up she can accommodate for it. You'll be helping her understand why changes in her life are difficult for her, and why she might feel increased anxiety whenever she's approaching some new situation such as starting a new school year, learning to swim, going on a family vacation, beginning ballet lessons, etc.

### "Why Can't We Do It the Old Way?"

**Six-year-old Adam has been accustomed to sitting with you in the front seat of the car while his baby sister sits in the car seat in back. Now his sister is old enough to sit in a regular seat, and, of course, she wants her turn sitting in that prized front space. Adam is livid and totally uncooperative.**

You could insist that Adam take his turn in the backseat, giving him a negative consequence (after you've returned from the trip) if he continues to throw a tantrum. If you hadn't thought to prepare him for this change in routine, however, it's fairer to let him have the favored spot until you have time to discuss the matter with him. Your choice of tactics is likely to depend on whether or not Adam has been uncooperative before the car ride. Once you've actually started the policy of turn taking, let Adam know that any scenes he creates in the future will automatically cancel out his next fair turn in the front.

It's always wise to prepare children for change *before* it happens. Talking with Adam about the fairness issue in advance, even getting his suggestions about how to implement the new ritual (flip a coin to see who starts off, magnanimously offer his sister the choice spot first to help her celebrate graduation from the car seat, etc.), would make all the difference.

Realize that Adam's difficulty is not just about riding in the front or back of the car. It's all about rivalry with a sibling and about the advantages and disadvantages of being the oldest. After all, he's had the distinct privilege of being the head honcho; when his sister gets equal status, he's bound to feel demoted.

When you talk with your child about such situations, point out the advantages of being "older" than a sibling. But save the speeches about his being able to "do everything first" *unless* he is already enjoying the privilege. For example, if he's already spending the night with friends, it's fine to point this out to him. But reminding him about being able to drive, date, and go to college first will have no real impact.

Basically, there are two things that make an older child feel that there's any real advantage to being older than a sibling: a later bedtime and an allowance (or a greater allowance)! These are privileges he can see in the here and now, and that's what makes them count.

### "I'M BORED!"

**You can't believe it! Nine-year-old Kelly has a new bike, a multitude of dolls, a shelf filled with books, a video you rented for her—not to mention a room full of toys. Now, as you sit down to get some work done, she stares glumly at you and once again complains, "I'm bored!"**

Go ahead and give Kelly a couple of suggestions about ways she might occupy herself. When that doesn't work, and it probably won't if she's frequently saying she's bored, *stop* making suggestions. Don't lecture her about how she could possibly be bored when she has every toy imaginable, or how ungrateful she is that she has all those toys and still complains. That won't work either!

Instead, give Kelly the message that it is up to *her*—and nobody else but her—to *'un-bore'* herself. In other words, she has a choice: She can sit around feeling miserable the rest of the day because she can't think of anything she's willing to do with her time, or she can pick something to do. It's that simple.

Of course, you might also let Kelly know that if she doesn't think of something to do within the next fifteen minutes, you'll be happy to assign her a chore. It's amazing how quickly she will discover *something* to do.

What you're teaching, of course, is that your child is responsible for coping with her own feelings. She can combat boredom by making a conscious decision to do something about it, not by waiting for a cloud magically to pass over her and zap her with a new feeling.

### "The Sitter's Mean!"

**You're tucking six-year-old Holly into bed when she suddenly announces that the person you've hired to take care of her is mean. Your gut feeling is that it's not true, but what do you do?**

Ask Holly to give you several specific examples of how the child-care person has been mean to her. Most often she'll relate incidents when the sitter, maid, or nanny, wouldn't let her do something she wanted to do (drink a soda) or insisted that she do something she didn't want to do (take her dirty dishes from the table to the counter). If this is the case, help Holly understand that the sitter is following your directions and does have the authority to make these decisions when a parent isn't around.

If your child accuses the sitter of doing something you consider to be abusive (slapping, hitting, shaking, etc.), let her know she's making a very serious charge. Make sure she understands the difference between telling the truth and lying, and then tell her it's very important that she tell you the truth about this situation. Tell her that you need to be sure that she's not just mad at the sitter and is trying to get that person in trouble. If your child's accusation seems convincing, your next step should be to talk to the sitter.

If you still have reason to doubt your child's accusation after talking to the sitter—and if your child is old enough to talk things out—you might bring your youngster into the room with the sitter and ask them both to discuss what happened. A child who's being manipulative is likely to fess up under the pressure of a face-to-face confrontation.

If your sitter has spanked your youngster, let her know that this is inappropriate. Even if you have decided to spank your child on occasion, it is inadvisable to give this power to any other caregiver. You could repeat your instructions about what you want the sitter to do when your child requires some type of discipline and give him or her a second chance. If the sitter continues to disregard your instructions, find another one. However, if the sitter has clearly lost control of her anger and acted very inappropriately (as in an overly harsh spanking or verbal abuse), you'll need to find an immediate replacement.

If your child was lying or exaggerating about the sitter's behavior, you'll obviously want to impress upon her the seriousness of such an accusation. Once you've done that, however, be sure to let her know that you do want her to tell you whenever she feels she's being mistreated in the future. You and she can sort the matter out together to see if something inappropriate is going on. If you don't make this clear, you child might be scared to tell you what's going on for fear you'll assume she's exaggerating.

Even if you feel fairly certain that your child's accusation was manipulative, it's wise to keep an eye (and an ear) on the interaction between the sitter and your child. Notice how your youngster acts around this person and check with each of them, separately, to see how they're feeling about each other.

Be alert to the fact that a child who's being treated harshly or being abused by a sitter might not tell you that this is happening. If you notice any regressive behavior in your youngster (unexplained tears, withdrawal, fearfulness, aggression, etc.) that cannot be otherwise explained, you'll certainly want to consider the *possibility* that the child has been or is being abused by a child-care person.

# CHAPTER 3

## *The Social Side*

If there's one thing that's sure to put a parent in the "hot seat," it's having her child behave in a way that brings disapproval from other adults. It can be especially painful if the parent is present when the child makes a social blunder or publicly misbehaves. Even the most confident parent is likely to feel pangs of embarrassment, guilt, or downright humiliation. She might worry as much about her own parenting ability (and what other people think of it!) as she does about her child's misbehavior.

Ironically, however, the first and most important thing a parent must do is develop a thick skin about how her child's behavior "looks" or "sounds" to other people. Difficult as it may be, a parent's main concern should be to provide guidance for her child rather than to worry about how she's stacking up as a parent in the eyes of others. If she's concerned, instead, with wanting to look "in control," she's likely to focus on stopping the child's annoying behavior in any expedient way rather than thinking about what the child needs to learn from the experience. In this process, she might humiliate the child and/or come on more strongly than her youngster deserves.

Equally distressing is to witness your child either being rejected or ridiculed by his peers, or treating his own pals poorly. Your heart aches for him because you know how much being accepted by his peer group and having friends will affect his self-esteem. If you see your child having difficulty with another youngster, you might be tempted to jump in and try to fix the problem. However, unless you have to step in to keep him from fisticuffs, it's usually better to let your child handle the social situation without your intervention and talk to him later about your observations and suggestions.

With these caveats in mind, let's take a look at some of the things kids do in a social or public context that can really make a parent feel "on the spot."

### The Tattletale

**Seven-year-old Marcie runs at breakneck speed to inform you that her younger brother has just sneaked a cookie out of the jar in spite of your making cookies off-limits right before dinner. She looks triumphant as she imagines the trouble that will befall her sibling.**

Calmly tell Marcie that you don't listen to tattles. Then resist your urge to say something about the matter to the cookie thief.

The point is, you don't want to reinforce the tattling. If you go ahead and discipline the guilty party—even though you admonish the tattler for her behavior—you defeat your purpose.

If Marcie protests your decision to say nothing to the offender, explain to her that nobody likes tattletales. If you had seen little brother stealing the cookie, or perhaps noticed the telltale crumbs on his lips, you would certainly call him on it. Since you didn't see either of these things, you're not going to let someone else get him in trouble.

However, make sure your child understands the difference between tattling and reporting a situation that should be reported to a grown-up. If a child is doing something that could be dangerous to herself or to other people (playing with matches), is injured or ill (vomiting or bleeding), or is committing a crime (stealing), these situations should *always* be reported to a grown-up as quickly as possible.

### The Poor Sport

**Your disgruntled ten-year-old Little Leaguer is standing in line with his teammates, waiting for the ritual handshake with the victorious team. But when the other team comes down the line, you see him deliberately put his hands in his pockets and refuse to congratulate the winners.**

Resist the temptation to talk to your child about his poor sportsmanship in front of the other kids or parents. As soon as he is alone with you, however, let him know how you feel about the situation.

You might begin by asking your child why he thinks you are allowing him to play a sport. Listen carefully to his response. Does it sound as if he thinks the whole purpose of playing ball is to win?

Let him know that, while it's fun to win, winning is not the goal (at his age). The real reasons you are encouraging him to play a sport are to learn the rules of the game, to learn about team spirit, to learn about fair play, to get physical exercise, to learn how to be a good sport, and to have fun. It's also an opportunity to learn how to get along with other kids as well as to admire the abilities of his peers. Winning or losing is not really the issue.

Explain that his refusing to shake hands with the opposing team is a no-no. People respect losers, but not sore ones.

You might also pause to reflect on the messages you send to your child about the whole issue of winning and losing. Sometimes, in our enthusiasm to get our youngsters to "do their best," we inadvertently influence them to feel guilty or inadequate if they're not first, "on top," or the winner.

### "I Have a New Playmate!" (But You Can't See Her!)

**You pass four-year-old Sara's room and hear her making conversation. Since you know that no one is in the room with her, you stop to see what's going on. You see Sara sitting all alone on her bed chatting away with an imaginary friend. Feeling a little unnerved, you wonder, "Is there something wrong with my child?"**

You might walk into Sara's room and say something like "Honey, are you having a conversation with a pretend friend?" If you don't act as if you think something is wrong, chances are Sara will tell you about her imaginary playmate.

It's perfectly normal for children—especially only children—to have one or more imaginary playmates. Fantasied companions are especially likely to crop up if a child is isolated from other children or has very few friends.

Imaginary playmates are of no concern as long as your child knows she's pretending. Once you've clarified that fact, you can be assured your child is not having an emotional problem. Youngsters usually outgrow these companions as they begin to make real friends. It's important, however, to respect the bounds of reality if you interact with these playmates. For instance, you might have a *pretend* tea party with your child and her imaginary playmate. It would be inappropriate, however, to set a place at the family dinner table for the fantasy companion.

Realize that many youngsters who have an imaginary playmate prefer to keep the details of that companion's personality to themselves. If a parent asks too many questions, the child might feel that her privacy is being invaded (the way you feel if someone aggressively insists on analyzing a dream you've casually mentioned). Better to let your child initiate the conversation and then be sensitive to her clues that it's time to end it.

Of course, if your child insists that a real person is present when nobody is around, or begins to be obsessed with including the imaginary playmate in every daily activity, consultation with a mental health professional is recommended.

### The Ungrateful Kid

**Your boss has come for dinner and has thoughtfully brought a birthday present for four-year-old Meg. The birthday girl excitedly rips the paper off the box, plunges through the tissue, pulls out a lovely outfit, and exclaims, "Yuck! I don't like this!"**

It's completely natural to feel mortified. According to adult standards, your child has behaved in a very rude manner. She's insulted your boss and seems horribly ungrateful and very spoiled. Even more disturbing, she seems an unfortunate reflection of your dreadful parenting skills. Here you are in an extremely uncomfortable position (and to think you'd intended to ask your boss for a raise next week!). The urge to punish your daughter on the spot, in full view of your boss (so he knows you're no pushover when it comes to your child), is probably overwhelming.

Don't do it. It will defeat your purpose. By adult standards, your child has been rude; by hers, she has been honest about a disappointment. A disciplinary action for this kind of "first offense" isn't needed. What you want her to grasp is the bigger issue about having consideration for other people's feelings.

First, apologize to your boss right in front of your daughter. It will be her first clue that something has gone wrong. "I'm sorry, Sam. I really appreciate your bringing the present. I need to talk to Meg about accepting gifts. You know how kids can be about these things." Then, calmly tell your child, "I understand that you were disappointed with the gift, but when someone gives you a present, you should thank him for it. I'll talk to you more about this later."

Then, try to put the incident aside and calmly proceed through the rest of the visit. It's not necessary to say anything more about it to your boss (who's probably also embarrassed) or your child (who will not benefit from continued grumbling about her terrible display).

When you and your child are alone, bring up her reaction to the birthday gift. Explain that when someone gives you a present, what you thank him for is his spirit of giving. Whether or not you like the gift is really beside the point.

Let your youngster know that a person who gives a gift is trying to please and to give something he thinks the recipient will like. If the person getting the gift says she doesn't like it, she will probably hurt the giver's feelings. "Mr. Smith was trying to do something nice for you. By telling him you didn't like that outfit, you could have hurt his feelings. It's a very rude thing to do."

You might also give your child an example she can relate to about being sensitive to other people's feelings. "Meg, let's say you drew a special picture for me in preschool and you couldn't wait to get home and give it to me. How would you feel if I looked at it, made a face, and told you I didn't like it? You'd probably feel pretty sad, wouldn't you?"

Don't just explain what your child *shouldn't* do. Tell her specifically how you want her to behave when she receives a gift. "You tell the person 'thank you' and you say something nice about the present."

Remind your child before occasions at which she will be receiving gifts about the proper way to accept them. Repeat these reminders until you're sure your youngster fully appreciates the sensitive and well-mannered way to behave. (And you might try using puppets for a little role-playing rehearsal!)

### "But It's Not My Fault!"

**Eight-year-old Sam is sitting in the family room. As his six-year-old sister walks by his chair, she trips and falls flat. Amid her screams, Sam immediately begins protesting that she was walking too close to him and his foot accidentally got in the way.**

Explain to Sam that, whether or not he intended it, it was *his* foot that tripped his sister. Therefore, it is his responsibility to apologize.

A similar example occurs when a youngster is playing with another child and breaks the other child's toy. Even if it was an accident, the child who broke the toy is still responsible for fixing, replacing, or apologizing for it.

The point is, it doesn't matter whether the problem was created by an accident or on purpose in terms of accountability. The perpetrator's intentions will certainly influence how people feel about him, but they don't change his essential social responsibility.

Many youngsters will try to affix blame on anyone but themselves. Even if an adult clearly sees them do something, they'll still argue that they didn't do it, that it was another person's fault, or that it was "just an accident." Many adults will back off when a child protests his innocence, especially if they didn't actually witness the event. But this tactic only allows a youngster to manipulate his way out of facing up to his responsibilities.

Rather than accusing the child of lying or making arbitrary decisions about blame, simply teach him that when he's involved in a situation, he must own up to his part in it. Tell him everyone blunders sometimes. Many children haven't learned, or been taught, that mistakes are only lessons, not evidence of inferiority, inadequacy, or "badness." If you can't feel okay about yourself unless you're perfect, would you want to admit that you made a mistake?

### The Car Pool Nobody Wants

**You're driving ten-year-old Barry and three of his friends to soccer practice. All of a sudden, chaos breaks out. The boys have begun some loud, physical horseplay that is driving you crazy and making it potentially dangerous for you to drive. You've told them several times to stop, but they continue to ignore you.**

Pull over and stop the car as soon as it's safe to do so. Calmly get out of the car and motion to all the occupants to do the same, lining them up side by side in a safe place. With a firm, nononsense voice, instruct your charges that you will not tolerate such behavior when you are driving because of the inconsideration for the driver as well as the danger both to everyone riding in the car and to everyone in cars nearby. Say something commanding like, "Now I'm going to ask each of you if I can count on your cooperation. Joshua, are you going to cooperate?" Making eye contact with each youngster, ask each, in turn, if he is planning to cooperate with you. Maintain your firmness and seriousness throughout this encounter, making it very clear that this situation isn't at all humorous, until you get a clear, positive response from every child.

After pausing and looking at the troops about thirty seconds after all have vowed their utmost cooperation, instruct them one by one to get back into the car. As you take the driver's seat, you'll probably have a pretty silent crew the rest of the way to the soccer field.

While this tactic wouldn't work if you used it frequently, the fact that you use it on rare occasions gives it a shock value that is very powerful. You are using a "potent parent" technique that demonstrates your control and authority.

If your child begins to act up in the car when the two of you are alone, your requests to get him to stop don't work, and you've warned him that your next step will be to take him home, it can be most effective to turn the car around and follow through with your declaration. When your youngster realizes what's happening, he might beg and plead with you to go to your original destination, but keep your resolve. The shock value will be tremendous.

Once you arrive at home, if at all possible (if there is an older child, another adult, or a readily available sitter at home) leave the child and go with your mate and/or other children to your original destination. If it's not possible to leave your child at home, give him a negative consequence for his misbehavior.

Of course, you might face a situation where you don't have the liberty of turning the car around and going home because you have to take your child with you to your destination. You could stop the car, say nothing, and wait for him to become quiet and cooperative before you proceed along your route. If this doesn't work, or he continues to misbehave once you begin driving again, make it clear that he will face a negative consequence once you return home.

### The Thief

**Five-year-old Ellen has been playing at a friend's house and you drive over to pick her up at the agreed-upon time. As the two girls say their good-byes and you get ready to lead your daughter out the door, she drops her purse. Out spill a couple of small toys and a bracelet that belong to the other child. The other mother and child register strange expressions while Ellen guiltily stares at the no-longer-secret stash.**

Of course, you're mortified! Although your first inclination might be to bolster your own image by expressing your outrage at your offspring, try to compose yourself as much as possible. Tell your daughter calmly but firmly, "Ellen, those things belong to Tiffany and you need to give them back to her right now." After she's returned the items, ask her to apologize to the other child and to the other mother for taking things that don't belong to her. You might also add, "I'm very sorry, Mrs. Jones. I obviously need to talk with Ellen about this."

Later, as you talk with your child about this behavior, emphasize property rights rather than focusing on the likelihood of your child's growing up to be a criminal. Realize that a preschooler might not realize that she's done something inappropriate. The message you want to give her is that you want her to learn from this situation and not repeat it.

In the next few months after this event, discreetly watch for any evidence that your child is stealing, especially when she's been around other children. If she does take something that doesn't belong to her, don't panic. Simply confront her firmly and insist that she promptly return any items to their owners. Be sure she carries this out by accompanying her or by getting a report from a responsible adult.

Since you know that stealing can become very serious (although many children will experiment with this behavior), set a negative consequence that will be in effect for several days after your child steals, assuming she was old enough to realize that she was stealing. You might consider not allowing her to have one of her favorite toys or items, pointing out how it feels to have one's personal property taken away. If your child has nothing in particular that she would miss, you could still set a negative consequence by taking away some privilege she values. Tell her that if she steals again, the consequence will be in effect longer. This gives a clear message that stealing is wrong, that you are wise to her actions, and that you will not allow this behavior.

You might wonder whether it wouldn't be enough just to reason with your child after she steals, making it clear that such behavior is inappropriate. The problem is that your words, no matter how wise, can mean very little unless you follow them up with action. This is why it's important to use a negative consequence when the problem first begins to surface rather than to engage in lengthier (and angrier) lectures.

If your youngster continues to steal, consultation with a mental health professional is recommended to get to the cause of this behavior. Children might take someone's belongings as an expression of anger or because they feel they are not getting enough adult attention, although their motivations usually aren't consciously conceived. A youngster who takes a parent's personal property may be symbolically expressing a wish to feel closer to that parent. Obviously, correction of the behavior problem will require addressing the child's underlying need to be closer to the parent.

## "But I Want *Designer* Jeans!"

**You're in the department store with ten-year-old Erica, standing in front of a rack of expensive designer jeans. She's fighting back tears and stoutly maintaining that she'll be totally humiliated if she has to wear any jeans other than the ones on the rack.**

While you may be tempted either to go ahead and buy the jeans (in spite of your best judgment) or to go home without *any* jeans, you might also consider a negotiation. Explain to Erica that you have only so much money budgeted for jeans. Therefore, she can either pay or earn the difference between the price of the expensive jeans and the price of the more reasonable (but not so popular) jeans, or she can decide to spend her budget for clothing on fewer new outfits and do her laundry more often.

You might wonder, "Well, why not just forbid her to get designer jeans under any circumstances and teach her that materialism and expensive fashion fads aren't something you approve of?" While this approach makes sense from an adult perspective, realize that preteens and teens are subject to tremendous peer pressure. Being accepted by "the crowd" might be important for your child's self-esteem. Also, would you want her to go in the opposite direction and dress in the style of peers who might be expressing counter-culture rebellion?

By giving her some option, you allow her to save face with her peers and to feel that you are trying to be on her side rather than against her. This is not the same as giving in to her every desire or allowing her to fill her wardrobe with expensive designer clothes. With this tactic, you're teaching her the healthy lesson that one cannot have what one wants without making choices and, sometimes, sacrifices to get it. Those designer jeans just might be worth the sacrifice to her at this point in her life.

### "I Won't Kiss Grandma!"

**Seven-year-old Steve is the apple of his grandmother's eye, and she's used to giving him a big kiss whenever she sees him. Now she's just arrived and is moving toward Steve for her usual greeting. Steve turns away, hunches his shoulders, and loudly says, "I don't want you to kiss me, Grandma."**

You don't know whether to feel sorrier for Grandma's hurt feelings or for your own embarrassment at your son's proclamation! Here you are having two problems: how to soothe Grandma's feelings, and what to say to your rude child.

One tack would be to kill two birds with one stone by telling your child, in front of Grandma, "Steve, you hurt your grandmother's feelings when you said you didn't want her to kiss you. The way you said it was rude, and you need to apologize to your grandmother for the way you spoke to her." You might also tell Grandmother something like "I'm sorry, Mom, I'm sure Steve didn't mean to hurt your feelings—it's just that he doesn't like kisses much anymore."

When you're alone with your child, find out why he refused the kiss. Is it because he's at a stage where he thinks kisses are for babies, even from you or any adult? Or is there something about Grandma's kisses that is objectionable to him (they're too wet, on the mouth, leave a lipstick print, etc.). If it's the latter, you might find a diplomatic way to let Grandmother know that your child doesn't mind a light kiss on the cheek, but that he has a thing about lip prints.

Let your youngster know that if he has a problem with something a grown-up says or does, there is a polite way to discuss the matter. He could say, "Grandma, I like for you to kiss me, but would you please kiss me on the cheek? I like that better" or "Grandma, please don't get your feelings hurt. I love you very much, but I don't much like kisses anymore. Could you just give me a hug instead?"

With a younger child who resists Grandmother's kisses but who is not old enough to articulate a reason or to negotiate a compromise, try to get Grandmother to understand that the child just doesn't like this type of physical affection from any adult other than, perhaps, his parents. This just might be a phase, but even if it's not, the child's behavior isn't to be taken personally. Tell Grandmother that you think it's important to respect your child's wishes about this so that the two of them will have a good relationship.

### "I Won't Play!"

**Nine-year-old Elizabeth has a friend over to spend the night. You hear the girls arguing about what to play, and suddenly Elizabeth screams, "I'm not playing with you anymore!"**

Call Elizabeth into a room where you can talk privately to her, and ask her what the problem is about. After hearing her out, explain in a no-nonsense, matter-of-fact voice that her friend is a guest and she doesn't have the option of ignoring her. Suggest, instead, that she negotiate a compromise with her friend.

For example, the two girls could take turns playing what each wants, perhaps flipping a coin to see whose turn is first. Or they could decide to do neither of the two things, but to find a third thing they could both agree upon. If negotiation doesn't work, tell Elizabeth she should acquiesce to her friend's wishes since the friend is a guest.

If your youngster begins a pattern of refusing to play with other kids when she doesn't get her way, you'll need to have a talk with her about friendship and about playing fair. Let her know that she could end up being very unpopular if she always has to get her way. There's a difference between standing up for your principles and beliefs and being an uncooperative kid who's a bad sport.

### The Kid Who Asks at the Wrong Time

**You've taken seven-year-old Hank to a movie. After you are seated and are waiting for the movie to begin, your son loudly asks, "Daddy, what's an orgasm?"**

Just keep your cool and calmly say, "Hank, that's a personal kind of question I'd rather answer when we're at home together. Remind me later, and I'll tell you."

Realize it's not the end of the world that your child has made an innocent inappropriate remark. Chances are the people in the neighboring seats will find the situation most amusing.

If your child makes other kinds of inappropriate remarks in public (such as talking about bathroom functions or subjects that might make some people queasy), just tell him that such topics are not to be discussed in public. Of course, it's best to teach this to your child at home, ideally *before* it occurs in public!

### The Restaurant Terror

**You look forward all day to going out to a family restaurant for dinner. It's a disaster from the moment you sit down at the table. Six-year-old Tommy bangs the silverware on the table as he awaits his food, talks too loudly, and spills his milk by being silly. After his food arrives, he's up and out of his chair, playing hide-and-seek among the tables.**

At the first offense, it's best to firmly tell Tommy that he needs to act appropriately. Remind him that "appropriate" behavior in a restaurant means talking in a soft voice, acting grown-up by sitting still, and staying in his chair until the meal is over.

But what happens if Tommy persists in his immature behavior in spite of your telling him to cool it? Excuse yourself and your child from the table and take your youngster outside the restaurant to talk, perhaps to the car. Let him know that you are very displeased with his behavior and will think long and hard before you take him to a restaurant again. If he is cooperative, he can return to the table with you.

If the situation is such that you are reasonably certain that a talk outside the restaurant will not work, pay for the meal and leave the restaurant immediately. While dramatic, it's rare that you'll have to do it a second time.

When you return home, reinforce your disapproval by following up with a negative consequence, such as an early bedtime. If your child has not eaten, let him have something simple but unexciting. In the weeks to follow, have a meal or two out when you do *not* invite your child to join you, with the message that you'll take him out with you again soon to give him a chance to prove to you that he's ready to act appropriately in a restaurant.

Realize that the best test of whether or not your child is ready to go out to eat in a restaurant is his behavior during meals at home. If he's having behavior problems, correct them at home before taking him to a public restaurant. If you can't get a babysitter and want to eat out, better stick to the carry-out places or to restaurants that cater to families with young children. It's just not fair to impose a misbehaving child on folks who are paying money for a peaceful meal.

### "I've Got to Win!"

**You're playing a board game with eight-year-old Johnny and suddenly notice that his playing piece has seemed to miraculously jump several spaces ahead of yours. Wanting to give him the benefit of the doubt and chalk it up to your poor memory, you say nothing. Then you spot him sneaking his man ahead a couple more spaces. When you confront him, he adamantly denies his behavior.**

Calmly fold the board game up and put it, and all its parts, back in its box. Tell Johnny that you won't play a game with him if he cheats.

Of course, if you're dealing with a four- or five-year-old, realize that he might not realize he's cheating. Calmly explain the rules when he makes an error and, with a sense of humor, say something like "Oh no, honey! We have to do it *this* way." And to keep his interest in the game, try to find a way to let him win fairly often.

Other versions of this having-to-win-at-any-cost strategy include the child who stomps off and refuses to play when he realizes he's losing, or the youngster who "accidentally" hits the board in such a way that the play is totally disrupted. And don't forget the child who refuses to play at all because of a fear that he can't win!

When your youngster has calmed down, talk with him about his game-playing philosophy. Ask him why it's so important for him to have to win a game. Point out to him that if he *did* win every game, nobody would want to play with him anymore because they'd have no chance to beat him. Both he and his partner would find such a game very boring.

Let him know that games are for fun, and many are based on luck rather than skill. Unless a person is participating in a very serious game competition, such as a chess tournament, winning or losing means nothing about the player—except perhaps that he got lucky.

Let your youngster know that a winner in life is a person who learns how to have fun, how to compete in a spirit of fair play, how to challenge himself by trying something new, and how to be a good loser.

### "Your Mom Gave You Away!"

**Ten-year-old Annette is sitting at the kitchen table with two friends, feasting on apple juice and chocolate chip cookies. As you go about making dinner preparations, you hear the girls beginning to argue. Suddenly, you're horrified to hear your daughter taunt her adopted friend with, "Well, *your* mom gave *you* away!"**

Call Annette away from the girls to a place where you can talk privately. Let her know that you heard her rude remark and are very upset about it. Insist that she return to the friend and apologize immediately. Suggest that she also say something like "I didn't mean to hurt your feelings and I really don't know anything about your adoption."

Later, when you and your daughter have time to talk, ask her if she understands why you were upset when you overheard her remark about adoption. Tell her that some youngsters are very sensitive about the fact that they're adopted, and they may have secret worries about why their mothers chose to give them to other parents.

Let your child know that a birth mother's decision to give her child up for adoption is usually an act of love. Because the pregnant girl or woman thinks she cannot take good care of a baby, which might be for a variety of reasons, she chooses to give the child to a family whom she knows *will* be able to give it the love and care it deserves.

Help her understand that making fun of a child for being adopted is similar to making fun of a child for being of a different race. Both are rude and hurtful to the one being teased or put down, and only reveal the narrow view of the person who makes such negative remarks. We are all people and we all move through life with different stories.

### The Kid Who Makes Embarrassing Remarks About Other People

**You're standing with six-year-old Billy in the ice-cream parlor waiting your turn to be served. He points to an obese lady at a table nearby and in a loud voice asks, "Mommy, why is that lady so fat?"**

You're not sure which is worse—your embarrassment about your child's remark or your anguish about the hurt feelings of the person your child offended. Although your wish might simply be to magically disappear through the floor, you're stuck right where you are.

In spite of the awkwardness, immediately tell your child, with as much calmness as you can muster, "Billy, lower your voice! Never point out someone in public and make a remark about that person's appearance (or behavior). It's very rude because your remark can hurt the person's feelings, even though I know you didn't mean to make fun of the lady." You might also tell that person, if appropriate, "I'm very sorry if my child offended you."

If it's any comfort, remember that children often embarrass parents by talking openly about their reactions to people who look or act different from the kind of people they're used to being around. Rather than dwelling on the horror of your child's remark, talk to him about the situation. If it's possible to converse about this at the time it occurs (without being overheard by the offended person), all the better. If not, be sure to bring the matter up as soon as you can comfortably talk to your child about it.

Not only do you want your youngster to become more socially acceptable, but you also want him to get the bigger picture about the need for consideration of other people's feelings. Explain that people who are overweight, handicapped, or have something unusual about their appearance or behavior often feel quite sensitive about it. To point them out, snicker, or talk openly about them can be very hurtful to them.

Help your child understand how such a person might feel by putting him in that person's place. "Billy, if you had something about your body that embarrassed you—maybe a really big scar on your face, or maybe something wrong with your foot and you had to wear a brace on it—you might feel bad about it. You wouldn't like people to point it out, right? Those comments make people think you're making fun of them and it hurts their feelings."

Let your child know that this same thinking applies not only to a person's physical appearance, but also to anything that sets that person apart. For example, the person might have a speech problem or not talk clearly and be hard to understand. Or the person might act strange because he has serious mental problems.

Let your youngster know that if he has a comment or question relating to another person in the room, he can quietly whisper his remark to you. Or he can tell you what he wants to say when the person is no longer around.

If a child persists in making offensive remarks within earshot of other people, give him a negative consequence when you get home (time-out, no television, no playing outside with friends, etc.). You'll be reinforcing your disapproval of his lack of consideration for other people's feelings. Also, ask yourself if your youngster might be expressing anger by trying to hurt someone's feelings. If you suspect this to be the case and the situation does not resolve itself, evaluation by a mental health professional can be helpful.

### "I'm Not Sharing This Toy with My Sister!"

**Your two girls, ten-year-old Melanie and eight-year-old Lynne, are playing in the family room while you're cooking dinner. Suddenly you hear Melanie screaming, "You can't have that doll! It's mine!"**

If the doll really is Melanie's, tell Lynne that she must give the doll back to its rightful owner. When an item is one sibling's personal property, the other sibling must have the owner's permission in order to use it. This is a different situation from one where a child has a guest over to play. In that case, she needs to learn to share her items with the guest (or to put them away before the guest arrives if she doesn't want the guest to play with them).

However, be sure to point out to Melanie that, unless she has a very good reason not to, it's really best to learn to share her toys with her sister. If she refuses to share most of the time, her sister's not likely to want to play with her or to be generous in return.

The point is, it should be the child's choice to share or not share with a sibling if the item belongs to her. But just as she shouldn't be forced to share, she must understand the natural consequences for not doing so.

It's also helpful to use such an opportunity to teach your youngster the arts of negotiation and compromise. Explain that the girls might want to decide to give each one equal time with the doll, or that Lynne be allowed to play with Melanie's doll while Melanie plays with something of Lynne's.

If you have two or more children in your family, it's important that each has some toys he or she controls. At the same time, it should be made clear that other toys and items are to be shared, such as the television, a doll house, an electric train, etc. All of the children will then have an opportunity to learn something about sharing—and about what happens if they refuse.

If two siblings begin arguing over a particular item that is to be shared and refuse to work out a peaceful solution, temporarily take away the permission to play with or use the item from both youngsters. When the two of them have reached a conclusion about how they'll solve the problem, one child can quietly tell you what has been mutually decided. At that point (but not before), you return their privilege of using the item. This tactic teaches children that it's better to share in the first place rather than to get caught up in an intense argument.

## The Child Who's Too Friendly to Strangers

**You're doing your weekly grocery shopping and suddenly notice that five-year-old Lacey has disappeared. As you scurry through the aisles searching for her, you spot her sitting at a booth near the deli chatting with a man who's having a cup of coffee.**

Walk over to the booth and say something like "There you are! I've been looking all over for you." Then, to the man, "I hope my daughter hasn't disturbed you." Take your child's hand, escort her back to the cart and resume your shopping. Tell her firmly that you want her to remain with you in a store and not run off where you can't find her.

That part's easy. The tricky part comes later when the two of you can talk and you let your child know the dangers of being overly friendly to strangers. How do you impress this upon her without frightening her excessively or teaching her to be an unfriendly person?

Begin by reminding her of the incident and explaining that, while the man was probably a very nice person, there are adults in the world who try to hurt children. If a child is very friendly to such an adult, that adult can take advantage of the situation and very cleverly trick the child into going off with him or her.

Let your child know some of the tricks such people use to lure children to a spot where they can be alone with or kidnap them. They might try to get a youngster to get into a car with them, or they might ask them to come with them to show them some baby kittens—and then grab the child and take them away with them.

Let your child know that it is fine to speak a little bit to a friendly stranger, such as saying "Thank you" if receiving a compliment, returning a casual "Hello," or answering a simple question ("Did your mother buy you that dress in this store?"), but that it isn't a wise idea to stop and get into a conversation with a stranger. Let your youngster know that if a stranger persists in conversation, to simply say, "Excuse me, my mother is waiting" (even if a parent isn't around).

Tell your older child that if she is all alone and a stranger approaches her to talk, she should yell, "No! Go away!" and run in the opposite direction. This shock tactic will usually cause the intruder to leave the child alone.

The best piece of advice you can impress upon your child to keep her out of a dangerous situation is: Never get into a car or go anywhere with any grown-up—even a familiar one—unless her parent has given specific permission for her to go with that person.

### "I Don't Like This Birthday Party!"

**You're sitting with the other parents at a child's birthday party and six-year-old Allison won't join the other children. A couple of times, the hostess has taken her over to where the other youngsters are involved in the festivities, but Allison either comes right back to your side or stands on the sidelines, refusing to participate.**

If Allison refuses to leave your side, try going with her to the group of children and staying near her as she joins in the activities. If she flatly refuses to participate once she gets there, you might put her on your lap and coach her in responding to the game, even doing the activity with her. If this fails, continue holding her, but move with the children as the different activities demand. For example, if it's time for ice cream and cake, sit with the group, your child on your lap or nearby. Encourage her casually a couple of times to eat, but don't demand or pressure. In other words, help her to participate passively rather than not at all.

Of course, you'll want to find out why your child doesn't want to participate. On your way home, ask her what the problem is. Then help her design a strategy for the next time she gets invited to a party, perhaps doing some puppet role playing with her to get her used to social interaction.

There may be other issues that are bothering your child. She might worry that she isn't properly dressed, or that she looks funny in what she's wearing. She might be afraid of a particular child who bullies or teases her. She might even be frightened of something that's going on at the party; for example, the clown might scare her, or she might hate noise and worry that the balloons will pop. A wise parent will talk patiently with her child to discover the specific reason the youngster feels so uncomfortable in these situations, and then give her appropriate advice or reassurance.

Of course, some kids won't participate in a party because they're being rebellious or angry. Perhaps you and she had a bad day up to that point, and she's paying you back by refusing to have fun at the party. If you suspect that this is the case and your youngster's attitude doesn't change after a few tries at getting her involved in the festivities, give her a warning that if she doesn't begin cooperating, you're taking her home. Then, follow through unless you see an immediate change in her attitude. If she says something like "I didn't want to go to that silly party anyway," realize that her statement represents a weak attempt to save face.

Of course, there are times when your child genuinely doesn't want to go to a particular party for some reason. Rather than forcing the issue, why not allow her to decline? There's really no need to create an issue unless the child's refusals become a habit, and your youngster will feel good about the fact that you do consider her feelings in making decisions which affect her.

### "Mr. Supersilly"

**You're cooking dinner when ten-year-old Max has an attack of the sillies. He giggles and squirms around the kitchen floor like a snake, oblivious to your requests to get him to stop. You're afraid that you'll trip over him and/or drop hot food on him because he's underfoot. Besides, you're tired of his testing you!**

Sternly give the squirmer a warning that he's going to get a time-out if he continues his behavior, and then follow through by sending him to his room if he doesn't comply. Let him know that he can come out of time-out as soon as he brings his silliness under control.

This tactic gives Max the message that you're interested in his learning to control himself. As soon as he does so, his consequence ends. He could go to his room, turn around, and come right back to the kitchen—*if* he's willing to stop his obnoxious behavior. Or he could spend a long time in his room before he decides he's ready to comply. The choice is clearly his.

You might also ask yourself if you've unintentionally contributed to Max's continuing silliness in any way. Often, a parent will encourage a child's silliness by joking around with him. Or a parent will admonish a youngster to stop behaving a particular way while smiling at the same time, giving an obvious double message.

It's important to be clear with your child when you ask him to stop behaving in some particular way. If you have been willing to be silly and joke around, but the child begins carrying matters to the extreme, be sure your message to "Stop!" also fits your body language, tone of voice, and facial expression.

### "But I Have to Be First!"

**You're watching eight-year-old Terry at soccer practice. To your amazement, you see him shoving another child aside during a drill, demanding to be the first to kick the ball. The other kid doesn't seem to mind, but you know Terry's behavior is wrong.**

There's not much you can do about this situation from the sidelines. But after practice, talk with Terry about his need to be first. As usual, you're likely to learn more about your child's motivation by asking some questions first. Why is it so important to him? Is he doing it in a misguided effort to earn your praise? Is he feeling jealous of other kids for some reason and this is his way of "beating" them?

In addition to talking about his reasons for his behavior, tell him that people—kids or adults—don't really like to be around others who are always needing to be first or to prove something. Let him know that, in competitive races, it's fine to strive to be first. But in most things in life, being first doesn't matter a bit. To help him understand this lesson, give him an example: "Remember when we went fishing last summer? We had a wonderful time, and it didn't matter at all who caught the first fish."

### The Constant Talker

**You're driving nine-year-old Judy to her ballet lesson and beginning to get a migraine. Judy, who's always very verbal, chatters away without any pause. You have something else on your mind and feel that you just can't listen anymore. But how do you keep from hurting Judy's feelings?**

Be up-front with Judy and tell her that, while you're interested in hearing what's on her mind, you just need a little quiet time at the moment. Explain that you're not in the right mood to be listening to her because you are preoccupied with something else and can't give her conversation your full attention.

So often, a parent will *half* listen to a child, especially one who always seems to be talking. The parent feels guilty telling the child not to talk, so she tries to look and act like she's listening, but she really isn't. The child responds by talking even more, sensing that the adult really isn't listening and hoping to get the point across by increasing the sheer volume of words (just like adults do when they lecture kids!).

It's much more efficient, not to mention honest, to tell a child directly that this isn't the best time to have a conversation with her. This truth will actually make her feel less rejected than if you listen to her halfheartedly. Give your explanation—which might be anything from not feeling well, being upset about something that happened earlier in the day, or just being very busy at the moment—and then tell her when you *will* make the time to talk to her (in thirty minutes, after you finish your paperwork, right after dinner, etc.).

Even though your child might be momentarily irritated that you don't want to talk, she'll learn—as long as you keep your promise to talk to her later—that you care about what she says and want to give her your full attention when she has something to tell you. This, in turn, keeps her from prattling on in an effort to get her point across to a half-listening adult.

### "I'M NOT TALKING!"

**You're with five-year-old Timothy in the mall and run into a co-worker. In spite of your friend's attempts to get Timothy to talk, he hides behind you, clinging to your leg and refusing even to nod or say hello!**

After a couple of attempts to introduce your child and enlist his participation in saying hello to your friend, ignore his shy behavior. If your friend persists in trying to get your son to talk, tell her something like "It's okay, Marsha. Tim's feeling kind of shy these days."

What many parents will do in this situation is to try to force the child to say or do something (shake hands, smile at the lady, and so on). In truth, these social conventions are learned from modeling adult behavior and are not to be expected from younger children. The parent who persists in trying to elicit these behaviors only gives the child a lot of attention. After all, he has two grown-ups focusing totally on him rather than on one another. What power!

Of course, you'll want to try to figure out just why your child might be acting this way. It might simply be that he hasn't had much experience in meeting adults, other than family members, and that he genuinely doesn't know what to do. It might also be that he's just shy by temperament and is going to need your patience before he's able to handle these situations with more aplomb. In any case, try using puppet play to model how you want him to act when you introduce him to someone. Before you go out with him again, have him practice his new skills as a reminder.

If your child has been getting a lot of attention, even though negative, by refusing to talk when introduced to someone, your best bet to decrease this power struggle is to give up trying so hard to get him to talk. If he doesn't respond appropriately when an adult speaks to him, matter-of-factly mention that he's been nontalkative lately, and then go on with your own conversation without any more references to his behavior.

### "I Don't Have Any Friends!"

**Nine-year-old Heather comes home from school looking very upset. As you try to get her to open up about what's troubling her, she suddenly blurts out a heartrending, "I don't have any friends!"**

Although your first protective impulse might be to exclaim, "Honey, that's just not true," hold off for a moment and practice your listening skills. Reflect her feeling back to her with a remark like "Gosh, honey, you seem so upset. What happened?" or "Well, tell me more about this, Heather. What's making you feel this way?"

But what if she refuses to talk, can't stop crying, or runs to her room and slams the door? Your job at this point is to provide emotional comfort rather than to focus on solving the problem. Put your arms around her, tell her you're sorry she's so upset, and stay with her awhile to show her you're there for her. Even if she's nontalkative for a time, just being with her in silence will be comforting to her.

When your child is ready to talk, you're likely to get a better handle on what's really going on between her and her peers. At that point, you'll be better able to target your response to the true situation.

If your daughter does, indeed, have friends, but is upset because a particular child rejected her or made fun of her, let her know that a person cannot be friends with everyone. Even friends get mad at each other sometimes and say hurtful things to one another. These feelings generally pass, the friends begin talking again, and things are back to normal.

But what if your child really does have a problem making

friends? Is she too shy to have the skills for forming friendships? Or is she doing or saying something which alienates her from other youngsters?

If she's too shy, let her know that there are several things she can practice doing with her peers and that will result in more friends. First, she can smile more often. Occasional smiles send the message that a person is not grumpy. Second, she can ask another youngster to share something with her (a toy, a project, part of her lunch, and so on). Third, she might learn to give sincere compliments. If she begins practicing these three things, her chances of gaining friends is very high.

If your child is doing something to alienate other children, it's very unlikely she'll admit it, even if she is aware of what it is. Trying to press your opinions will just make her defensive, withdrawn, or angry.

Instead, suggest that the two of you sit down and create a list of all the things kids do that other kids don't like. Give her some ideas and encourage her to add to the list. Your list might have some things on it like tattling, being a crybaby, being bossy, starting fights, putting other people down, not playing fairly, always having to have the last word, acting unfriendly, and so on.

After the two of you have exhausted the possibilities, ask your child if she ever has done any of the things on the list. She'll probably mention one or two things; if she doesn't, gently remind her of a couple you or other grown-ups (teachers, coaches, etc.) have noticed. This is an effective nonblaming approach to helping her recognize her own weaknesses, at which point you're able to talk to her about how she can overcome them. You might also share a time with her when you did some of these behaviors, helping her to feel less upset with herself.

### "But They All Tease Me!"

**Nine-year-old Clayton comes home from school fighting back tears. He says the kids are calling him awful names and that nobody likes him!**

You probably have a good hunch about why Clayton gets teased, so explain it to him: "If you let kids get you upset and explode or cry, they know they've found the perfect way to get to you." But, even though you explain this until you're blue in the face, chances are Clayton won't change his troublesome behavior. You're probably going to have to *actively* teach him how to respond to teasers and bullies.

You might be tempted to teach him to simply "ignore" the kid who makes fun of him. But this tactic rarely works unless it's done the first few times a child is teased. By the time teasing has become a problem for a youngster, his peers will persevere in torturing him even if he is able to carry off the ignoring act for a short time.

Instead, give your child some comebacks for the bullies. He might say, "Cut it out!" or "Oh, grow up, Larry!" or the sarcastic "Yeah, right!" and then walk away. But he'll need to say these remarks confidently, not like a wimp. So help him practice with role playing until he looks and sounds the part!

### The Unfriendly Host

**You and a friend are chatting on the couch while four-year-old Thad and your friend's four-year-old son are playing nearby. It becomes obvious that your son is being extremely bossy with his guest, demanding to play only what he wants and ignoring his friend's wishes. The other little boy is quite passive, allowing your child to dominate him.**

If Thad were a little older, you'd call him out of the room to talk to him privately about his bossiness. But preschoolers generally don't resent your correcting them in front of a peer.

Say something to Thad like "Thad, you need to let Ben have a turn deciding what to play. He'll think you're a better friend if you let him decide sometimes," or "Thad, Ben won't want to come play with you if you continue to order him around." If Thad continues his behavior, give him a "time-out," just as you would if he'd done something inappropriate and you didn't have company. If your friend says something like "It's okay, you don't need to punish him," just tell her that you'd rather handle the situation in your usual fashion. She'll probably respect you more for taking effective action.

If your child continues to be rude to or uncooperative with your friend's child, acknowledge your disappointment to your friend and apologize to her for your youngster's behavior.

If your child's bossiness of other youngsters is a recurring problem, consider using a treat (special snack) or privilege (extra bedtime story) to reward "friendly" or "cooperative" behavior. Remind him to allow his friends to have a turn deciding what to play just before he enters a social situation with other children.

### "It's My Turn to Be on Your Lap!"

**As you sit down on the couch, three-year-old Brandon and five-year-old Cliff both scramble to get onto your lap. You know they're vying for your attention, yet you're a little annoyed that your older son won't let your younger son have a little time with you. But how do you handle this without showing favoritism?**

Although you could set up a turn-taking system, this can get complicated as you try to remember throughout the day who sat where last. Instead, you might try telling both youngsters, in a good-humored sort of way, that you've got a terrible problem: two wonderful boys you love to hold, but only one lap. Then, let each one sit beside you for their hugs. But if you've really spent more time with one of the boys that day, you might explain to the other, "Look, Cliff, Brandon hasn't had much time with me today. Let him sit on my lap for a little while, and then I'll play with you a little later."

You know, of course, that what you're really dealing with is good old sibling rivalry. As your children get older, they'll be keeping track of who gets the most "time-outs" in a week, who gets to play video games the longest, or who gets the most jelly beans in his Easter basket. Prepare yourself for the fact that they'll probably be vigilant about noticing anything you do that might smack of unfairness!

One of the best ways to keep sibling rivalry to a minimum is to spend time with each child *separately* on a regular basis. Most parents know this, but feel overwhelmed wondering how on earth they could ever put this into practice, given their busy lifestyles.

Actually, it's quite easy, provided you think in terms of *very short* time periods (ten or fifteen minutes daily per child). To put this plan into effect, tell your youngsters that each will have a "special time" each day (if possible). For example, if you have two children, "special time" could be just before bedtime for the youngest and a little later for the oldest. For families with schedules that change every day, the youngsters can be told at breakfast when their "special time" will be for that day.

To make this work, these time periods should be spent doing something the child wants to do, within appropriate limits. She might request a back rub, a story, being pushed in the swing, having her hair brushed, playing a game, or just talking about a topic she's picked. It's not a time to discuss discipline matters or anything unpleasant, unless the child brings such issues up for discussion.

"Special time" can work miracles in lessening sibling rivalry. After all, it gives each child the gift of your undivided attention.

# CHAPTER 4

## *Aggressiveness*

All parents want their children to behave in socially acceptable ways. They know that inappropriate aggressive behavior is a problem in any setting. Kids who are overly aggressive can cause tremendous trouble for themselves and others. And, of course, if you raise your child to value nonviolence, his aggressive behavior can be especially disconcerting.

If your child is overly aggressive, ask yourself what circumstances may be going on in your family or home that might prompt his angry feelings. Has a new baby recently arrived? Is there marital tension in his environment? Has someone been ill and required more of your time and attention than usual? Have you been preoccupied with problems of your own? Has there been a loss in the family, such as the death of a grandparent, or a divorce?

What about *your* style of releasing anger? Parents, after all, are a child's first models for expressing (or repressing) any kind of feeling. It's going to be very difficult to convince your child to contain his hot temper if yours is out of control.

Realize that it's very important for you to give your child *appropriate* methods to release his anger. Parents are pretty good about telling kids what *not* to do when the child is angry: no spitting, hitting, kicking, breaking things, and so on. Often, however, parents forget to tell youngsters what they *can* do. They can talk about their feelings ("I don't like that," "I'm mad"), they can release their anger through drawing or writing, or they can engage in some physical activity (active play, riding a bike, throwing throwable objects where nothing can get broken, beating up on a pillow or mattress).

Now that you've speculated about what might be causing your youngster's aggressive actions and have some ideas about how to help him appropriately release his angry feelings, let's look at ways to handle some specific "hot seat" situations.

### "I Hate You!"

**You've been arguing with seven-year-old Justin all morning about one thing or another. Finally, you've had it with his obstinate mood, and you tell him he's just lost his television privileges for the day. To your horror, he shouts, "I hate you!"**

Acknowledge Justin's anger while making it clear that you're not changing your mind about the discipline. For example, you might say something like "I know you're mad, Justin, but you still lose TV tonight!" Or you could use a little humor, said nonsarcastically, with "Honey, next time they have a sale on mothers, you can trade me in on a better model."

The point is, don't overreact to your child's use of the word "hate." Realize that he's not using it in the adult sense; if adults seriously hate someone, they are usually expressing an intense negative feeling that doesn't easily change. But when kids use the word "hate," they mean it in the same way they'd say, "You're a turkey!" Their negativism is usually short-lived and is just an impulsive angry statement, nothing more.

Obviously, you will want to give your child more acceptable options for expressing anger. When he's calmed down, let him know that to say "I hate you" really hurts your feelings and is also a disrespectful way to talk to an adult. Tell him, "When you're angry at me, it's okay for you to say, 'I'm mad at you,' 'I don't like that,' or 'I think you're being mean,' instead of using the word "hate."

Some parents are so shocked when a child says, "I hate you," that they give in to the child's wishes, punish him more, or change their minds about the consequence they've already set. This tactic simply teaches a youngster that he now has a weapon whenever he wants to get his way with that particular parent!

### The Biter

**When you pick up four-year-old Katy from day care, you feel a little panicked as the director motions you into her office and closes the door. She tells you that your daughter has been biting children and that she wants to discuss steps you both can take to help Katy.**

First, ask the director to describe the situations in which Katy bites a child. Does it seem that she's biting because she's angry (another child took her toy) or because she might be trying to get attention (a group of children are playing and she walks over and bites one of them)?

Once you've listened to what the director has to say, share any information you have (Dad just moved out, a new baby has arrived, and so on) that might help explain why your youngster might be biting. Then assure her without being defensive that you will work on this problem with your child. It might help to remember that the director is likely to be nervous about this discussion. She doesn't want to get complaints from other parents, but she doesn't want to lose your business either. Also, many kids go through a biting phase and still grow up to be wonderful adults. So don't panic in fear that your child is becoming antisocial or is otherwise disturbed.

The next step, of course, is to talk things over with your daughter. If you think she's biting because she wants to join in with other kids but doesn't know how, role-play with puppets to show her how to get positive attention from her peers ("Can I play with you?" or "May I look at that with you?" etc.). If you decide she may be angry, give her some other ideas about how she can express those feelings with the other children. Teach her that it's acceptable to say something like "I'm mad because you took my blocks!" or "I won't play with you if you keep doing that," or "Cut it out! I'm playing with that now!"

If a talk with your youngster corrects the situation, count yourself lucky. Usually, you have to add other measures to ensure that the biting stops.

You may need to give your child *appropriate* substitute behaviors for expressing anger. For example, she could make angry scribbles or drawings on construction paper, she could throw something soft (foam or stuffed animals) at a designated target, she could pound on her pillow, and so on. She could also be given something acceptable to bite in order to redirect or diminish her need to bite.

Be clear with your child that biting people is an absolute no-no. It hurts the person who gets bitten, and it's not a safe way to play.

If these measures don't work, you might try arranging a simple incentive system with your child's teacher at the day care. If Katy goes for one day without biting, she gets a star (a smiley face, a check plus, etc.) to show you when you come to pick her up. Then, make sure the teacher's reward counts for something. For example, the star might earn Katy an extra story before bed, thirty minutes of time to see her favorite video, or reading in bed for fifteen minutes after her normal bedtime. It doesn't matter what the reward is as long as the child finds it motivating and it's acceptable to you.

If the teacher tells you that your child did (or tried to) bite someone that day, the biter earns a negative consequence. It might be not seeing television that evening, having an early bedtime, not being allowed to play outside that day, and so on.

This approach gives your child the clear message that both you and her teacher are united in a common cause to eliminate the biting. It also lets your child understand that you and her teacher communicate and that she can't play the two of you against each other.

You might wonder if the time-honored solution of "Bite her back and let her see how it hurts!" would be appropriate. The problem to consider, however, is what this strategy teaches your child about aggression. Your child will get the message that when you get in a bind, you'll do something physically hurtful to prove your point—and that perhaps, so should she.

### The Kid Who Hits a Parent

**Since Brian was about two years old, he has indicated his displeasure when you do or say something he doesn't like by hitting you. Now that he's five, his hits are beginning to hurt. Not only that, but you wonder what other people think when they see your child hit his own mother. You've just made him angry, and he is now charging at you. You're determined to put an end to this pattern right this minute!**

If at all possible, grab Brian's hand to prevent him from hitting you. Firmly tell him that you will no longer allow him to hit you and that if he does it again you will give him an automatic time-out. If he does hit you again, give him the time-out *immediately* without allowing him to beg, argue, or change your mind with promises (unless you are in a public place, in which case you would give him the time-out as soon as possible).

It's quite common for a parent to think some particular behavior is "cute" when the child is a baby or a toddler. The same behavior, however, is no longer "cute" in an older child. It's much better to teach your youngster right from the beginning—no matter how young he is—that hitting you, or any other adult, is totally inappropriate.

Sometimes a child will act as though he's hitting a parent "for fun," when in fact the parent suspects that the child is expressing real anger. When you grow serious he might say, "It was an accident!" or "I was teasing!" Let the child know that you really don't believe he was teasing. Besides, teasing is allowed only if both parties are finding it fun. If one person doesn't like it, it's not teasing. Rather, it's mean.

Tell your child that you think he's angry with you about something and that he is afraid to tell you what it's about. Encourage him to explore with you what the source of his anger might be. Whether or not the two of you figure out the cause, let him know that you will no longer consider his hitting you to be any form of teasing, and that he'll earn a time-out for this behavior.

### THE TANTRUMER

**You are in the kitchen cooking dinner with four-year-old Robert nearby. Suddenly, he's into the pantry looking for the peanut butter. You remind him that dinner is in thirty minutes and that no snacks are allowed. At that point, Robert throws himself to the ground, yells and wails, kicks the floor, and thrashes about like a wild animal.**

You have a couple of effective choices. You can either walk away and ignore the screaming beastie, or you can send him immediately to his room, carrying him if he won't go on his own. If you pick the latter method, let him know that he may come out of time-out as soon as he's ready to control himself.

The problem with the first choice is—let's face it—it's terribly hard to truly ignore a tantrum! You'll have a better chance if you are in a position to leave the room, but if you're a captive audience, as when you're cooking, it's almost impossible to truly ignore a screaming child. You might *think* you're doing a good job of ignoring him, but if you're going about your work with a little extra intensity or force, if your face is turning red, or if you're slamming the cabinets shut, your child will read you like a book. He'll know that he's getting exactly what he wants (next to getting that peanut butter!), which is to rattle you and to get you upset.

A time-out in the child's room (or some other area, such as a utility room off a kitchen) makes it impossible for the child to know if you're being rattled or not, since he can't see you. This method gives him no attention at all, which is why it's usually more effective than trying to ignore the tantrum.

Many adults waste their time trying to argue, cajole, or change a child's mind while the child is in the midst of a temper tantrum. Just as it's difficult—if not impossible—to argue with a person who's very drunk, it's also pointless to try to reason with a youngster while he's throwing a tantrum. Talking to him only reinforces his power by giving him what he wants—your complete attention.

### "But I Didn't Mean to Hurt the Doggy!"

**You're glancing out on the patio, keeping a watchful eye on six-year-old Jimmy. Suddenly, you're horrified to see him hitting the family dog with a tree branch.**

"How could *my* child do such a thing?" might be your first thought. You and your spouse are loving people. You treat your son with compassion, and you've made sure to teach him to be gentle and kind to animals. Does this mean your child has a mean streak you've never noticed before? Is there something wrong with him?

Not at all. This kind of behavior in young children toward animals is quite common. It is not an indication of any deep-seated emotional problem, unless it becomes a chronic pattern.

Whether you think your child is unaware of the effects of his behavior, or you suspect he's venting some anger, deliberately or otherwise, your first priority is to stop his actions as quickly as possible. "Jimmy! Stop that right now!" will send a clear, firm message as you quickly get to your son to retrieve the branch. Continue with an explanation: "You must never hit an animal unless it's attacking you. You could hurt Pooch by hitting him like that."

After making sure your dog is not injured, talk to your child about the proper treatment of animals. Point out that he would be very upset if someone hit him with a stick, pinched him, picked him up by one leg, or any number of other unkind things kids do to animals.

If being around an animal is a new experience for your child, your explanation should suffice. However, if he's already been warned about rough or cruel treatment of a pet, realize he's probably displacing some anger. Ask him if he's angry about something, pointing out that his behavior suggests that he is. Of course, he might not realize he's angry, or, even if he knows he is, he might not know why. If you can, help him figure out the source of his frustration and give him options for venting it. If neither one of you can establish the probable source of the anger, at least you've taught your child that his behavior is an act of aggression. In any event, make it clear that he must not be mean to a helpless animal, and keep an extra sharp eye out for what might really be upsetting your child.

Sometimes a youngster will be cruel to a pet under the guise of loving it. For example, in a supposed attempt to hug a pet, he might squeeze it too tight. Or he might act like he's petting the animal but be pulling its hair or knocking it off-balance. If this happens, confront your child directly about his behavior. "Jimmy, you're hurting Pooch when you hug him like that! If you're doing something that hurts him or that he doesn't like, that's being cruel." In other words, correctly define your child's behavior for him rather than playing along with his explanation by saying something like "Well, Jimmy, when you love Pooch, be more gentle about it." The child's behavior is not loving, it's hurtful, and he needs to face this fact.

To reinforce the seriousness of the situation, you might also want to set a specific time period during which your youngster will not be allowed to play with a pet. "You're not allowed to play with Pooch anymore until after supper, Jimmy. Then we'll see if you're ready to play with him in a gentle way."

## The Destroyer

**You're sitting in the family room watching television and relaxing after dinner. The remote control falls to the floor and, as you reach to pick it up, you notice that the leg of the coffee table has your eight-year-old Lewis's initials crudely scratched into the wood!**

Call Lewis into the room and point out the initials. If you have more than one child, be sure to determine which one actually did the deed. Once you know Lewis is the guilty party, let him know that you're furious because there is no excuse for carving on furniture (since he's old enough to know he was damaging property).

If the carving was done by Lewis's scissors, have him give them to you. Tell him he can have the scissors again when you think you can trust him not to damage property or, perhaps, after the damage has been repaired. In other words, temporarily confiscate the item he used to cause the damage, whether it be crayons (drawing on the wall), a kitchen knife (cutting something that shouldn't be cut), or some toy that was used to create the problem (hammering dents in the tile floor with the end of a metal truck).

If your child breaks or damages something that can be fixed, let him be instrumental, if it's appropriate, in doing the cleanup work or in fixing the damage. In the coffee table example, you might have him sand the table leg and help put on the wood stain.

If the property can't be fixed at home, or if it requires that a repair person comes to fix it, consider having your child pay for some or all of the cost. If this isn't practical, you might assign your child some special chores to "work off" his debt. If it's practical, make the chore something that is related to the incident—in the case of the coffee table, dusting or polishing furniture.

Of course, you'll want to talk to your child about the value of property and about the disrespect involved in deliberately defacing or breaking it. To help him relate to this, ask him how he'd feel if someone damaged his favorite toy, his bicycle, or something else that he treasures. Make sure he understands that the financial cost of the item is actually beside the point—it's just as inconsiderate to carve on a worn piece of furniture in your house as it is to deface a brand-new piece.

### "She Did It!" "He Did It!"

**You're trying to have a serious conversation with your mate when you hear seven-year-old Melissa and her eleven-year-old brother, Jack, getting into loud horseplay in another room. Suddenly, a screaming Melissa appears to show you a scratch on her arm, wanting you to punish Jack for hurting her.**

Send both combatants to their rooms immediately. Melissa is not seriously hurt, and you know from experience that both youngsters were probably responsible for the horseplay.

What many parents do in such a situation is to sit down with the two culprits and have each give a description of "what happened." No matter how fair the parent tries to be, the fact is that one child is going to feel unfairly treated if the parent takes sides (the one who is declared the guilty party!). The other child, of course, will be quite smug.

Also, unless you've actually witnessed the entire scene, you really can't tell what happened. Each child is going to give you his or her *perception* of what happened, not necessarily the truth. And the truth is that each child probably contributed to the problems.

Typically in sibling hassles, the younger child needles the older child unmercifully until the older child gets fed up and does something physical to the younger child. Then, because the older child became physical, the parent punishes him ("You are older, so you should know better!") and lets the younger child go scot-free.

A fairer disciplinary action is to punish *both* (or all) youngsters involved in the dispute. Rather than trying to play judge and jury, the parent should give the clear message that she's not going to get caught up in the kids' argument. If the two of them want to play together, it's up to them in most cases to work things out between them. Obviously, if you witness a physical act of violence by one child toward the other—*and you were also there to see that the victim did nothing to the aggressor*—you would give only the offender a negative consequence.

To help prevent such problems with siblings from occurring in the first place, try to nip things in the bud when you first hear your youngsters getting inappropriately loud. Walk into the room where they are arguing or roughhousing and, unless one is crying or you see physical blows being exchanged, say something like "Kids, this is a warning. Keep the noise down," or "Okay, gang, let's keep things down to a dull roar. If I have to speak to you about this again, you're going to have to separate." If you see one or both hitting or shoving, or if one is crying, immediately send each to a separate room for a specified length of time.

Many parents notice that their children fight constantly, except when the parents aren't home. Then they seem to get along great! The fact is that many siblings fight because it gets them parental attention, although they are probably unaware of their inner motivation. They can be getting along well, cooperating, and playing together when the parents are on an errand—but then begin arguing as soon as their parents pull into the driveway! The lesson from this is that unless you have a troubled child who is excessively aggressive and physical with a smaller or weaker sibling it's very unlikely that either will get seriously hurt in their squabbles.

In other words, allow your youngsters to work out their own solutions to their problems whenever possible. If they get too loud about it, warn them that if they don't quiet down, you'll separate them. If one is already screaming, separate them immediately.

But what about the situation where one child really is hurt, such as when kids are getting physical and one ends up with a broken arm? Obviously, your first job will be to tend to the injury and get appropriate care. But then what do you do about the hurt and angry feelings of the victim and the guilt of the offender?

Sit both youngsters down and ask them to tell each other how they feel about what happened. The point here is to get each youngster to realize that it was not the offender's *intent* to seriously injure the victim, and that it is also totally normal for the victim to feel angry and hurt about getting injured. Ask the offender to apologize to the victim, if he doesn't do it spontaneously. Then, let each child be aware of the obvious lesson in this situation:

Roughhousing and/or physical conflict can end up with someone getting hurt. Be sure to help the offender deal with his guilt by assuring him that you know—even if he was very mad at the sibling—that he did not really intend such a serious outcome.

### The Taunter

**Ten-year-old Reese has a mouth that constantly gets him in trouble. This afternoon, a neighbor calls to tell you that Reese is no longer welcome on her property because of his making loud, obnoxious put-downs to the other children who had gathered to play in her backyard. As you put down the phone, your thoughts are "Now I've had it!"**

First, get yourself calmed down before you confront Reese. Obviously, you'll plan to give him some negative consequence for his inappropriate behavior (possibly to include writing a note of apology to the neighbor), but give yourself a little time to think this out before you say anything.

Then, calmly tell Reese what the neighbor told you and listen carefully to his response. After all, you do want to hear his side of the story. You also want to listen to him to determine whether he's cocky, nonplussed, or remorseful. If he doesn't much seem to care about his behavior, you'll need to impress upon him your anger not only about what he did, but also about his lack of concern. But if he's feeling guilty and in obvious distress about his actions, you can be softer in your approach.

The more difficult job might be to figure out why your child is making these aggressive remarks. Is he feeling badly about himself, and trying to compensate for his lack of self-esteem by putting peers down? Is there some reason why he's carrying around a lot of anger? Does he think he's being funny and isn't tuned in to social cues? Is he modeling his behavior after someone in the family? Obviously, you'll need to address the underlying problem in order to see any long-term change in his behavior.

Of course, you'll talk to your youngster about how other people feel when they are the brunt of put-downs and aggressive remarks.

But it might be very difficult to help him understand the impact of this type of behavior without input from the "victims."

If you think your youngster is developing a habit of making aggressive remarks or put-downs to his peers, consider checking with the school, community agencies, or private mental health practitioners to find a social skills group for your child. These groups can be enormously helpful (in a fairly short period of time) in getting youngsters to understand the effects of their behavior on other people. The group leader can "stop the action" whenever a child is inappropriate in group, and then can ask for feedback from the other kids. This kind of confrontation by *peers,* under the supervision of a trained leader, will often convince the offender to change his ways.

### The Child Who Deliberately Hurts Herself

**Eight-year-old Tammy is upset because of an "F" on her report card. You've talked to her about ways she can improve in the next grading period and made it clear that her "F" isn't the end of the world. Still, she's mad at herself as she goes off to her room. A few minutes later when you take her a snack, you find her sitting on her bed making small scratches on her arm with the tab of a soft drink can.**

Immediately go over to Tammy and express your shock and dismay at what she's doing, not in an angry way—but with great concern. You want to give her a clear message that you consider her behavior to be extreme and very inappropriate. Even more, you want her to know that you never want her to do anything to hurt herself, no matter how angry or upset she might be.

Tell Tammy that no matter how angry a person gets—either at other people or herself—a person should never do something to hurt herself. In the first place, everyone makes mistakes. In the second place, there are many other ways to release angry feelings that aren't hurtful to anybody.

If she's mad at or disappointed in herself, help her explore her guilty feelings. Is she worried that family members are disappointed with her? What else might be going on that is making her feel bad about herself? Help her put all this in perspective, pointing out that there's *nothing* she could do that would justify physical aggression upon herself. Hurting inside, whether she's sad or angry, doesn't justify her attacking her body. If she feels she needs to be punished for something, she needs to talk about these feelings with a parent (or other responsible grown-up) and get feedback about what she might need to do to feel better.

If she's angry at someone else, give her suggestions about appropriate ways to release anger. Let her know that it's perfectly normal to get angry, especially at family members and other people you love. But give her a very clear message that doing something aggressive to herself is absolutely not acceptable.

If your child has actually hurt herself (a cut rather than a scratch), see a mental health professional, even if the behavior has occurred only once. If her effort to hurt herself was very superficial, such as a light scratch, watch carefully to see if she ever repeats this kind of self-abuse after you've made it clear that it's unacceptable. She might have just heard about another child's doing this and was being experimental. But if it occurs again, seek professional help.

## "I'll Do It" (But Then I Won't!)

**Before going out for the evening, you remind eleven-year-old Jenny that it's her night to do the dishes. When you come home, you find the dishes done, but the dirty pans and silverware are untouched. The next day Jenny nonchalantly explains, "Well, you said to do the *dishes*; you didn't say anything about the pans or the silverware!"**

If this is the first instance of Jenny's literal translation of the dishwashing assignment, you might laugh and congratulate her on her getting one up on you! Then explain that you intend in the future for her to consider the *intent* as well as the content of any future assignments.

However, if Jenny tends to be passive-aggressive (seeming cooperative and agreeable on the surface but not following through with appropriate action), chances are she'll have other areas where she'll show it. She might clean something up as you've requested, but make a bigger mess while doing it. Or she could continue to promise that she'll get something done, yet never actually carry it out. In other words, she'll continue to find ways to sabotage herself in getting a job done yet act as if she's cooperating or as if you're simply being unreasonable not to appreciate her efforts. Unlike the aggressive youngster who will defy, challenge, or argue with you, the passive-aggressive child will promise you almost anything (or at least, not refuse you openly) but will deliver almost nothing.

Two strategies can help counter passive-aggressiveness. The first is preventive: Give your child specific instructions with clear deadlines. Have her repeat your instructions back to you, or give them in writing, so there's no arguing about what was said or not said. Then, don't nag. The second strategy occurs after the fact: Insist that your child pay the consequence for *not* doing what you've asked no matter what her excuse. Continue to keep your youngster accountable for the *intent* of your words, particularly if a "second offense" is involved.

While it's normal for youngsters to occasionally show passive-aggressiveness, kids who do so habitually are expressing anger, rebellion, or resentment—but without taking any responsibility for having these feelings. In fact, they might even deny these feelings to themselves (even though it's clear to everyone around them!). Somehow they haven't learned that it's okay to express such feelings. This may occur because someone else in the family is modeling this behavior. Or perhaps they are being overly controlled by a parent to whom they don't dare show their anger. In some cases, they might have parents who have told them that they are not allowed to disagree with or express anger to adults. And, if a parent has a bad temper or uses corporal punishment, a youngster will quickly realize that passive-aggression is the only safe kind to show.

Obviously, the way to prevent serious passive-aggression in your child is to let her know *appropriate* ways to disagree and to express anger with adults, and for you as an adult to send a clear message that you're willing to *talk* things through. If a parent is aggressive or rejecting to the point where the child feels helpless, the youngster may resort to passive-aggressive responses.

# CHAPTER 5

## *School*

As you reflect on your own childhood, you probably have very strong memories—positive and negative—about school. After all, the majority of your waking hours were spent there five days a week, nine months of the year. Whether pleasant or painful, school was bound to have had a significant impact on you.

Not only did you spend a great deal of time in school, but much of your self-image as a child depended upon what went on there. The ease or difficulty of the work had a lot to do with how smart you (or your parents) thought you were. Your popularity—or lack of it—with your classmates had a lot to do with how you perceived yourself socially. And the attitude the teachers took toward you had a lot of influence on how you felt about yourself. In addition, your attitudes toward achievement, authority, and learning were greatly influenced by your experiences in school.

With the advantage of hindsight, is it any wonder that parents are very concerned about how their kids feel about school? Consider, too, the common pressure *parents* feel around the school issue. When your child goes to school, he is judged according to norms for other kids his age. Will he measure up? Behavior you've allowed or tolerated might not be considered appropriate by his teacher. For the first time, you might hear some criticism of your child that you don't like, agree with, or want to admit. Your own ideas of your child's intellectual capabilities might not prove accurate.

Also, your child may be exposed to ideas and values that you don't agree with. You might not approve of the teacher's methods or curriculum, yet are unable to do anything to change them. You might begin to feel that you are losing some control over your child and his life.

Then, too, there's the frustration you'll feel when your child is struggling with any school problem. Your heart will ache for his sagging sense of self-esteem as he wrestles with work he's having trouble understanding, tries to cope with a classroom bully, or experiences ridicule about his appearance.

So it's no wonder that emotions may run high between you and your child when it comes to school. As both of you quickly realize, there's a lot at stake.

But a parent need not overreact. Kids—and their classes and teachers—change every year. Most teachers are genuinely interested in your child's progress, and are approachable if you have a question or a concern. If your youngster develops a problem either academically or socially, there are many ways for a teacher, counselor, or parent to help. Even more comforting, kids change. What might be a problem one year might not crop up the next.

Now let's take a look at some of the common situations that can put a parent in the "hot seat" when it comes to the matter of school. And remember, if you try to make sure that your child does everything "right" (and doesn't repeat your own errors!), your unrealistic approach is only *creating* a "hot seat" situation for yourself!

### "Don't Leave Me Here!"

**You've prepared five-year-old Jake well for that important first day in kindergarten. As you walk into the classroom, Jake's teacher warmly greets him at the door and you see your big boy readily joining the group of children. Then suddenly, as you're about to leave, he runs over and clings to your leg, wailing at the top of his lungs!**

Calmly reassure Jake that he'll be fine and tell him when you'll see him next. Gently hand him to his teacher so she can keep him with her while you matter-of-factly walk away. Even if he screams louder, continue walking and leave the school.

As cold and unsympathetic as this might sound, most youngsters will stop crying within a few minutes of a parent's departure. Just ask any experienced kindergarten teacher.

But what if your child is one of the few who doesn't stop crying for some time? Just let the school handle the situation. Why? Because if you remain with your child and try to soothe him until he stops crying, he'll probably cry longer. After all, he will have your total attention and will quickly figure out that the way to keep you nearby is to continue his fussing. Also, staying with him will only subtly reinforce his feeling that there really must be some reason for his fears—otherwise, why wouldn't you leave?

Keep in mind, too, that many children who are quite accustomed to preschool, day care, or baby-sitters will surprise a parent by having separation problems that first day of school. Although you've prepared your youngster well for this big day, there's likely to be some anxiety for *both* you and your child. After all, this day is a psychological marker for your child's leaving the world of toddlerhood and officially entering childhood. He's "in school." It's the Big Time. In fact, if the parent doesn't readily leave, it's fair to say she might be having a separation problem of her own!

Many a mother has a hard time allowing her youngster to move out of babyhood. She might be afraid of losing control over her child. She might be being overprotective or using closeness with that child to fill some void in her own life. A child has emotional radar that will inevitably pick up the mother's true feelings. Sensing the mother's anxiety, the child may become frightened and want the mother to remain in the classroom. The child's behavior makes it appear that the child is having the problem when in fact it's the mother's problem!

So leave your child at school even when he's protesting. You'll be giving him a clear message that you know he'll be safe there and that you are comfortable with his taking this step toward independence.

Of course, it can help minimize your child's anxieties about starting school to spend some time preparing him for that important first day. Many schools have an "orientation" day for kindergarten before the start of the school year, when both parents and kids can see the child's room, meet the teacher, and see the child's classmates. If your school doesn't offer this, take your child to the school before it starts to at least familiarize him with the school entrance, the playground, and any distinguishing features of the school building. If you can, talk to your neighbors, or to parents of other youngsters who go to that school, to find out what you can about the class your child will be entering. You usually can call the school a week or so before classes officially begin to find out the name of your child's teacher, what pets might be in that teacher's classroom, or any other information that might help your child know what to expect on that important first day.

Also, children often feel more comfortable if they can take something to school that makes them feel connected to their home and familiar things. A favorite toy, a small object, or a picture of a parent tucked into a pocket or backpack can do the trick.

Many kindergartens are now allowing parents to stay with their children for a part of the morning on the first few days of school. This child-oriented approach makes psychological sense, since an expectation that most five-year-olds can separate abruptly from a parent is unrealistic (even if the youngsters have been to preschool). Parents may want to become advocates for their local kindergartens having a more age-appropriate orientation.

**"My Tummy Hurts!"**

**You've been having trouble getting nine-year-old Veronica to school in the mornings. She wakes up with a pained look on her face and complains of feeling ill, but never runs a fever. The pediatrician says he can't find anything physically wrong, and that the problem is stress-related. This morning she's once again complaining, "My tummy hurts!"**

Take Veronica's temperature. If she does not have a fever, insist that she go to school. Certainly, you can go ahead and give her any medication your doctor has told you is okay, but tell her she must absolutely go to school.

If your child complains of nausea, give her a large Ziploc bag to keep in her backpack, purse, or pocket. Tell her that if she's worried about not making it to the rest room to throw up, she'll have the bag "just in case."

It would be better, of course, to have talked to Veronica in advance about the fact that unless she has a fever she'll go to school no matter how uncomfortable she feels. Whether in anticipation of the "next tummy-ache day" or after the fact, explain to your child about stress-related symptoms. Make it clear that you're not saying she's lying to you or that the symptoms are "all in her head." Although there are kids who will malinger in order to get permission to stay home from school, many youngsters do, in fact, suffer stomachaches, headaches, nausea, and other maladies that are very real even though they are stress-induced. Even if your youngster gains some advantage from not going to school, it doesn't mean she's deliberately conjuring up her physical symptoms.

Let your child know that being worried or emotionally upset can cause a person to get a stomachache, headache, or other ailment. And all of us, even adults, have times we don't feel up to our usual par; yet we still go to work and carry out our usual responsibilities. We might not know what is troubling us, but the headache or stomachache is the way our body lets us know something's not quite right with us.

Of course, you'll want to problem-solve with your child to see if either of you can figure out what's bothering her. Common causes of kids' developing ailments that could keep them home from school are worries about tests or grades, being teased by peers, being embarrassed about changing clothes for physical education, avoiding some competitive situation, or feeling overwhelmed or intimidated by a teacher. It's also common for youngsters to develop stress-related physical symptoms if they are worried about a parent or about family problems (Mom and Dad are divorcing; Mom is depressed, so I need to be here to cheer her up; my baby brother gets to stay home during the day).

The point is, however, that the child needs to go to school whether or not you've figured out the problem that's causing the difficulty. By reassuring her that you sympathize with her discomfort, but by also insisting that she continue her usual routine, you teach her a healthy way to cope with such problems as an adult.

To help prevent your child from using "illness" as a way to stay home from school, examine your behavior when you *do* allow her to stay home. It's helpful to make a few ground rules. For example, some might be that you don't go anywhere, except to a doctor, when you stay home from school, even if you feel wonderful after four o'clock. If you stay home from school, you cancel all after-school and evening plans. Also, a day home from school is a quiet one, with restricted activity and diet according to the sickness. Although it's appropriate to give a sick child some extra nurturing and care, you don't want to overdo it with presents, favorite meals, or constant entertainment.

### "I'm Not Going!"

**Wondering why eleven-year-old Molly hasn't yet appeared for breakfast, you go to her room. She's still in bed and declares, "I don't want to go to school."**

Your first job in this situation is to differentiate between the child who might legitimately need a day off and the youngster who is having a more serious problem. Some parents—and teachers—believe in an occasional "mental health day off" from school. Before you consider this, however, you need to think about how many absences your child has already had, if any, as well as your child's need to be in school that day. Will she be missing anything important? Is she having problems keeping up in one or more of her subjects? Do you have a sneaky suspicion that her bid to stay home "just this once" is hiding some deeper problem with going to school? Answering these questions will help you determine whether or not to allow her to stay home, even if you believe in the "mental health day" idea.

If you know, or suspect, that your child is beginning to have a problem about going to school, your job is to get her to school. Give her reassurance and support, but insist that she go.

Of course, your child is likely to tell you that she just doesn't want to go to school *that* day, but will promise to go the next. If you were to allow this state of affairs to continue several mornings in a row, it's highly likely that you would realize that—no matter what Molly is saying—she's not going to go to school on her own. This is why it's important to do everything in your power to get her to school as soon as you realize she's developing a problem. This might mean calling your spouse, a relative, or a friend to come to the house and matter-of-factly insist that the child go to school. A youngster will often acquiesce if her father or another adult appears on the scene.

Unless your child is small and you can easily carry her into the car, do not try to physically force her. It's much better to call in support to prevent injury to yourself or to your child.

Once your child is in the car, realize that she might refuse to get out of the car after she's arrived at school. If this happens, ask if the school can help. Often the principal, counselor, or a teacher will come to the car and escort the child into the school building if he or she knows you are having this problem. Many youngsters will enter the school without incident at that point.

If nothing works and you cannot convince the child to go to school—or if she has to be physically carried into the school—make an appointment with a mental health professional. Be sure to tell the person doing the scheduling that your child is refusing to go to school. That information should get you an immediate appointment, as school refusal is considered an emergency by professionals who work with children and adolescents. Why an emergency? Because a child's refusing to go to school—in spite of the measures just mentioned—usually will not stop without professional intervention to evaluate the emotional dynamics behind the child's behavior. Also, the longer the child is out of school, the more difficult it will be to get her back in.

### "Will You Help Me with My Homework?"

**At nine o'clock last night, eight-year-old Kevin—who should have been in bed a half hour earlier—was sitting with you at the kitchen table laboriously writing sentences from his new list of spelling words. Somehow, twenty minutes of homework had stretched into three hours, and your patience had worn thin. Now it's tonight, and Kevin is due to start his homework. Already you're feeling tense.**

It's time to wean Kevin from having to have you sit with him while he completes his homework. After all, you've already been through third grade.

Check with Kevin before he starts his homework assignment to see if he understands what is expected of him. You might watch him do the first problem or write the first sentence. If he's not understanding, help him figure out what he needs to know. Then leave him alone, telling him to come show you his work when he's finished the entire assignment. If Kevin can't even begin the assignment because he hasn't done the appropriate background reading in his book, show him where to read and then leave him alone.

To help this process along (since Kevin will probably do everything in his power to sabotage your efforts to get him to work independently), ask Kevin how long he thinks it will take him to do an assignment if he gives it his total, undivided attention. Make sure he sets a realistic goal, and then set the timer for that amount of time. Getting him used to setting appropriate goals—and then meeting them—is a good way to motivate him to focus his attention.

If this method doesn't help, you can add an incentive system. Tell your child that if he finishes by the time the timer dings, he'll earn an incentive (or a "point" toward an incentive). Remember that incentives can be special together-time with you (reading, playing a game, cuddling, and so on), not necessarily television, special snacks, or the eventual earning of a toy. However, remember that an incentive won't work unless it's motivating *to your child,* and some youngsters will not respond to the promise of some activity with a parent.

When your child gives you finished work, check it for *completion* rather than accuracy (unless he's clearly misunderstood the entire assignment). You might let him know which items are wrong, if any, but leave it up to him to correct his work. After all, the teacher needs feedback about what your child doesn't understand. If you "help" your child to turn in perfect homework, how will the teacher know where he's having trouble? So resist your own perfectionistic tendencies.

If your child wants to do his homework in an area where the whole family is gathered (or in the same room as you are), allow him to do this *only* if he works and doesn't dawdle or get distracted. A few nights of doing his homework in his own room, or some other isolated place within the house, might make him eager enough to return to his favorite spot by getting his work done promptly.

If your youngster resists your attempts to get him to work independently by refusing to work at all, deny one of his privileges (watching television, using the computer, riding his bike, etc.) until he does his homework at the appointed time. Remember, though, to get his input about the time of day he prefers to do his homework. Some kids want to do it immediately after school "to get it over with"; others want to relax, play, and unwind a bit before tackling their homework. You can often gain a child's cooperation about homework simply by giving him a choice about when to do it.

Remember a simple rule about helping kids with homework: If either you or the child is crying or yelling when you're helping with homework, it's best to find someone else for the helper role. Try switching parents for this task, or perhaps ask an older brother or sister to help out. If this isn't possible, consider taking your child to school early—or letting him stay after school—for school-sponsored tutoring sessions. Some families have even hired neighborhood teens to come over for forty-five minutes or an hour to serve as a homework "tutor." If you decide to use this method, be sure the teen doesn't actually do the child's work for him.

Realize that many youngsters will appear to "need" a great deal of parental help with homework as long as it is freely offered. After all, can you think of a better way to get a parent's attention all to oneself almost every evening? Of course, a parent needs to make sure that a child has plenty of parental attention at other times.

### The Child Who Doesn't Pay Attention

**The teacher tells you that six-year-old Daniel is having problems in first grade. He doesn't pay attention, doesn't follow instructions, and is beginning to bother other children by talking and wandering around the room. She suggests that he's just immature, but she wants you to talk to him about paying attention and doing his work.**

Unless your talking to Daniel changes things significantly, arrange for him to get a complete educational evaluation (either through the school or privately). This will include testing of his intellectual ability, achievement levels (math, reading, spelling), perceptual-motor coordination, and language processing.

The reason you'll want this testing done is to *rule out* possible learning differences and/or attentional problems in your child. Teachers will often label a student as "immature" or "rebellious" if he doesn't do what is asked of him in class. Or they might assume he's having family or emotional problems. While any of these notions might be true, the fact is that many youngsters who act as if they don't care about schoolwork are actually having genuine attentional or learning problems.

It is especially easy to miss such difficulties in bright children. If a youngster is quick in math, reads well, or has an excellent vocabulary, the teacher might assume—because of these capabilities—that the child has no learning problem. Interestingly, bright children often give up quicker on a task than more average youngsters. They simply assume that everything should come easy for them, so, if they have a learning weakness, they just stop working. The teacher often concludes that the child is just being noncompliant rather than questioning whether or not there is an underlying learning or attention weakness.

Of course, it's also possible that your child's classroom might be too regimented, given his age, that a teacher's expectations for conformity might be unrealistic, or that he is not being challenged. Evaluation requires that all aspects of a child's school experience be examined.

If your youngster does have a learning difference, there is help available. Many schools have programs where a child can get extra help from a specially trained teacher during the school day. There are also private clinics that provide interventions for learning problems. A call to the education department of a university or college near you can supply you with information about these sources.

If professional evaluation reveals that your child is having problems paying attention, possibly because of hyperactivity, it can be most helpful to consult a mental health professional about ways you can help your child. Common approaches include behavior modification, dietary changes, and/or medication.

Learning and attentional difficulties will typically surface during your child's first few years of school. Early diagnosis is important not only to give your child the best educational programming for him, but also to preserve his self-esteem. Left undiagnosed, many children with learning and/or attentional problems develop emotional or behavior problems as a result of their frustration with school. While you would obviously work on your child's behavior in either case, professional evaluation is essential before you assume that his problems are the result of immaturity or emotional/behavioral issues.

### "What Homework?"

**When you ask nine-year-old Dustin why he never seems to have any homework, he tells you that he gets it all done in school. Then comes the report card, bearing low grades and the teacher's comment: "Not completing assignments!"**

First you'll want to check with your child about why he's not doing his homework. Is he not understanding the work? Is he having a problem with his teacher? Does he need help organizing himself so he can remember to bring his assignments home? Would it help for him to write his assignments on a special pad, which you could check daily? Talking with the teacher, hiring a tutor, or helping him organize his notebook more efficiently might help. Help him decide on a strategy to correct the problem, and then see if he'll work it out independently.

More typically, however, the primary problem is not one of the above, but rather the child's general lack of motivation for doing schoolwork. In this case, you need to ask youself about the *cause* of your youngster's motivation problem. Is the school's program not challenging him, or perhaps not approaching him through his best learning style? Is he having a learning difficulty that has not been diagnosed? Is he depressed? Is his lack of discipline a way to rebel against you?

It's especialy important to look for emotional causes for your child's drop in grades or refusal to do schoolwork if he has typically done his homework and gotten good grades in the past. Sudden changes *might* indicate a serious depression, drug use, sexual abuse, or other significant problems. Encourage your youngster to tell you what's really bothering him. If that doesn't work, or you're not sure how to handle the problem that surfaces, seek professional help.

But how do you manage the problem of your youngster's lack of motivation? An effective approach is to arrange a system with the teacher that lets you know if Dustin is getting his homework done on a *daily basis*. For example, in his notebook, assignment book, or on a piece of paper, have Dustin write, "I turned in all my homework from yesterday." The teacher simply initials this statement if true; if it's not true, she'll probably note any assignment that's missing. Dustin's evening privileges will depend on his having a positive note—and remembering to bring it home! If he doesn't bring the note, or if the teacher marked a missing assignment, he may have to forfeit television, the phone, the computer, his usual bedtime, or something else he'll miss. This system also lets you know on a nightly basis what assignment, if any, he still needs to do. When your child shows consistent improvement for several weeks, you can switch to a weekly reporting system with weekend privileges as the incentive.

But what if your child forgets to bring home his books? You can deal with this problem in a number of ways: You can help him set up a system for remembering to bring home the books by linking this to some other activity he does every day before coming home ("When the teacher starts writing the next day's assignments, I'll remember to get out my books"; "When I get my coat, I'll remember to get my books", etc.); you can get him in the habit of bringing *all* his books home every night and give him an incentive for that; or, in the case of a very disorganized child, you can enlist the teacher's help in reminding him about his books. Some parents have found that a visual signal, such as having a piece of brightly colored yarn on his backpack's zipper, will remind a youngster to put his books in that backpack.

For kids who resist doing homework, it also helps to have a rule such as: If homework is not done by 7:30 P.M., everything else stops until the homework is completed. If the child is eager to see a television show at 7:30, he'll need to start his homework earlier. Otherwise, he'll miss anywhere from ten minutes of the program to the entire evening's selection, depending upon how long it takes him to finish his assignments. This tactic prevents the parent from having to nag the child, since nagging usually only increases a youngster's resistance to doing his schoolwork.

In addition to these strategies for solving your youngster's homework problem, you'll still need to address the fact that he's been lying to you. Talk with him about the fact that the most serious consequence of his behavior is that he has violated your trust. Let him know that trust, although easily broken, takes time to earn back. While making it clear that it will take some time before you can again trust him about the issue of homework, be positive about the fact that you do expect him to regain your trust.

### "I Cheated"

**Ten-year-old Lisa arrives home from school with a long face and a note in her hand. You can hardly believe your eyes when you read the teacher's message: Lisa was caught cheating on a test!**

Instead of going ballistic and threatening to ground Lisa until she's thirty, acknowledge the disappointment that she must be feeling to have to bring you such a note. Then set aside time as soon as possible to talk with her.

Start out the conversation by simply asking Lisa to tell you what happened. Was she copying from someone's paper, or was she allowing someone to copy from hers?

If Lisa was doing the copying, your goal is to find out why she felt she needed to cheat. Is she afraid she won't get a good grade and that you'll be angry with her or take away her privileges? Is she afraid she'll lose her place on the honor roll? Is she responding to a dare? Does she think cheating is wrong, or does she think it's okay because "everybody does it"?

If her cheating was based on fears about what you would do if she made a bad grade, let her know what you *would* do. Depending on the circumstances, you might do nothing, you might insist that she set up a "study hall" until she brought the grade up, or you might even take away some privilege until her grade improved. In other words, give your child a realistic picture of what you would do, but make sure she knows that low grades would not be the end of the world—or the end of your love for her.

In addition to telling her how you would handle her making a low grade, let her know how you would *feel* in such a situation. Ideally, your feeling would be concern rather than anger or disappointment. Even if you know you would be angry (because she told you she had studied and really hadn't), reassure her that this would certainly not change your love for her.

If your youngster cheated because of her own high expectations of herself, let her know that she's over-emphasizing the importance of grades in her life. Although it's nice to make the honor roll or straight A's, grades are never a measure of a person's worth or smartness. In fact, many very smart kids make mediocre or poor grades because they aren't willing to expend the effort to make good ones.

If your child's attitude about cheating is that it's "no big deal," let her know that she's wrong. Cheaters rob themselves of really learning the material they should have studied. Even more important, they have their own conscience to deal with. Even if nobody else has caught on that a person made a good grade because of cheating, the person herself knows. And if a person continues to do things that are deceitful, she will eventually feel very bad about herself.

If Lisa was not doing the copying, but allowed another child to copy from her paper, you'll want to know why Lisa is afraid to say no to the person who invited her to be an accomplice. Chances are she's afraid to displease this person. Perhaps this peer carries high status in the class or is one of Lisa's good friends. Maybe the peer made some threat to her, or even bribed her.

Talk with Lisa about personal integrity. Let her know that a person who rejects a friend because that friend doesn't do whatever that person wants is no friend. It's important for a person to learn to stand up for what she believes is right, even if it displeases some people. Help your youngster learn ways to turn down an invitation to cheat; for example, "I'd like to help you out, Margo, but I just don't want to cheat. Besides, we could both get into a lot of trouble, and I don't want to risk it." Point out that she can offer to help her friend with schoolwork, but in a different way, so her friend knows she cares.

Sometimes a youngster who's accused of cheating will insist that she's innocent. If this is the case, encourage her to talk with the teacher. Chances are that if she normally tells the truth, the teacher will believe her. Offer to go with your child to talk to the teacher about this, if your child wants you to. Respect her right, though, to handle the matter herself if that is her preference.

If this is the first time your child has cheated, let the consequence the teacher gives (probably a "zero" on her test) stand on its own. Having had a good discussion with her about cheating may ensure that she won't do it again. If this is a second (or worse) offense, set a negative consequence (loss of privileges for a week or so) for her at home in addition to the penalty given out by the teacher.

Incidentally, many of the same issues for cheating also apply when a youngster changes a grade on a report card. Faking a better grade is, after all, another form of cheating.

### "I Got into a Fight!"

**The teacher calls one evening to report that nine-year-old Jeff had been fighting with other children, sometimes even hitting them. You assure the teacher you'll do something about this problem, hang up the phone, and then wonder, "Now what on earth do I do?"**

Obviously, you'll want to talk with Jeff about his aggressive behavior. Although hitting is out, it's important to know if your child is being harassed or ganged up on by other kids. If so, have a talk with the teacher to alert her to what is going on. If you find that your child is provoking these fights, that's good information for you to know and to discuss with Jeff.

If this is the first time there has been a problem with fighting and your child is not being victimized, give him a clear message that his actions are inappropriate and that you'll be checking with his teacher regularly to make sure the problem isn't recurring. In such a case, however, chances are high that you've heard this same complaint before! Talk with the teacher about the possibility for setting up a behavior-modification program for Jeff in which you coordinate your son's behavior during the school day with his privileges at home. Many teachers are open to this idea, even with an older child, if you suggest it.

There are many creative ways to implement such a system (for any school behavior problem), but let's look at a generic program that you can modify to fit your own circumstances. Consider a "card" system where the teacher gives the youngster a green, yellow, or red card at the end of each day. The green card indicates that the child had a great day—showed no aggression with peers; the yellow card indicates that the youngster might have been mildly verbally aggressive, but was still within the limits of general appropriateness; the red card meant that the child was physically aggressive or markedly verbally aggressive.

When the child returns home from school each day, he shows the parent the card he earned for that day. The parent then implements the appropriate reinforcement: green card equals a special privilege (later bedtime, falling asleep to a radio, time on the computer, etc.); yellow card equals a "normal" night; red card equals a negative consequence (early bedtime, no television, no playing outside, etc.). As always, it's important to find out what constitutes a positive reward or privilege to your child, so consultation with him is essential.

Teachers usually like such a system because it doesn't require writing notes and it takes very little of their time. Obviously, stickers, different colored stars, "happy" versus "frowning" faces, or even a "check-plus, check, or check-minus" reporting system can be used rather than the colored cards. Some teachers prefer a two-level system in which the child either earns a privilege or a negative consequence—with no middle ground.

If a child has several teachers during the school day, a simple form can be made upon which each teacher can give the appropriate mark for the youngster's behavior. For example, if all his teachers give the positive mark, the child earns the privilege; if not, he earns the negative consequence. If the child's problem is only occurring in one particular class, you could use this system just for the particular class period. (Of course, you would also want to determine why your child is having the problem only in that one class.)

If you decide to use this type of behavioral system for your youngster's school conduct, be sure to work out the details with the school counselor or your child's teacher. Most teachers are familiar with such systems, and might have good ideas about tailoring the program to the particular needs of your child.

You might wonder if using a system of this kind would be deterimental to your child, thinking that all the fuss calls his classmates' attention to his problem. In truth, the kids in the class *already* know your child has this problem. A behavior-modification system, handled matter-of-factly and without shaming by the teacher, should not lead to embarrassment.

You might also wonder why you would want to allow a child to earn special privileges for behavior that is expected in the first place (not fighting)! After all, we expect youngsters to behave appropriately in school because they want to please their teachers and parents and because they don't want to get into trouble.

While this conventional strategy usually works for the majority of kids, there are some children who, for various reasons, remain unmotivated by the usual structure. Behavior modification can work quickly, but it works best if youngsters are given a "good faith" boost by being able to earn privileges or incentives *in addition* to experiencing negative consequences for inappropriate behavior. Allowing a child to earn something positive is less punitive than using only negative consequences, and makes it more likely that a rebellious or angry child will be interested in modifying his troublesome behavior rather than rebelling even further.

But what if your child doesn't want to cooperate with such a system? If he strongly protests the idea, you might give him one chance to show you that he'll behave appropriately so that no such system need be implemented. If the behavior happens again, then you start the system as planned. However, most youngsters in elementary school like such systems as long as they can earn privileges or incentives that are important to them (later bedtime, getting to have the dog sleep on their bed, video game time in the evening, etc.).

The advantage of using behavior-modification systems with school problems is that the child gets a clear message that his parents and teacher(s) have the same expectation and that they are, in fact, communicating. The child who's struggling to find his sea legs in school knows that his teacher and parent will work with him and help him set limits he can't seem to set yet for himself. They will look for problems that may underlie the behavior, not just punish or nag him. And for the child who is manipulative, such close teacher-parent communication will make it less likely that the child can "do a number" on either the parent or the teacher.

Certainly, if a younster's aggression presents a physical danger to other children or, if it becomes chronic, consultation with a mental health professional is strongly recommended.

### The Underachiever with Great Potential

**School achievement test results are in, and, as you suspected, eleven-year-old Michael is in the ninety-ninth percentile across the board. His teachers have told you every year that he is very bright and has great potential. But he barely maintains a C average—and couldn't care less about academics!**

First, you'll want to check with a physician to rule out the presence of a physical problem (anemia, thyroid disorder, and so on) with your child. Next, ask yourself if he's overscheduled. Or is he bored because he's not getting the necessary educational stimulation he needs? Would an outside course in something he's very interested in motivate him to improve his school performance?

Is there some psychological reason for your son's minimal efforts in school? Is he depressed? Are there family problems? Has he suffered some abuse? Is he rebelling against you? If you suspect any of these issues, professional counseling can be helpful.

You might also encourage your child to make better grades by starting a system where he earns or loses privileges based upon his academic performance. For this plan to work, however, the youngster must be very motivated to earn the privilege.

Unfortunately, it's not always possible to pinpoint a "reason" for your child's underachievement. Your best efforts to improve matters might not work. Frustrating as it is, your youngster's underachievement might just be something you'll have to accept. As the old saying goes, "You can lead a horse to water, but you can't make him drink!"

While you'll certainly want to do everything possible to help your child perform at the top level of his capability, there might come a time when it's wise to take a different tack. Your "new" approach would involve letting your child know that you know he's smart and capable, and that one day he'll find himself interested in something which will jump-start his motivation. When that time arrives, he'll begin to take his studies seriously. In the meantime, consider his efforts in school, and his grades, to be in *his* control and let him take responsibility for his achievement (or lack of it).

Realize that the critical factor in this approach is that you continue to give your child the message that he *will eventually* find something that will motivate him to study and to find learning enjoyable. There should be no aura of parental resentment, criticism, or terrible disappointment hanging over the child. This tactic is quite different from that of the parent who "gives up" on the child and remains angry with him, even though no longer pressuring him about grades.

Also, you can continue to search for challenges that will motivate your child even though they are not considered "traditional" academics. Mechanical problems (things to fix), museum visits, camping trips, exposure to music and art, and other enriching experiences can stimulate your child and perhaps plant a seed for a later vocational or recreational interest.

If you use this second approach, your child might not "bloom" until middle school, high school, or even the beginning of college. He might even drop out of college for a while (or never even start!), but might then "bloom" and return to school with a new sense of purpose and probably will do very well. Many successful adults have followed this nontraditional path.

So if you've used the more traditional tack and it isn't working, consider switching. True, your youngster won't get the scholarships, and you won't be the parent of the valedictorian or get to be in the audience at his National Honor Society installation. But you also won't have as many tears, arguments, resentments, and headaches. Is it really worth giving up a good relationship with your child in order to hassle him constantly about homework and grades?

### "The Teacher's Wrong!"

**You're having a nice evening relaxing and watching television when the phone rings. It's the teacher calling about eight-year-old Monica's poor academic or social performance. When you confront Monica with the news, she tells you that her teacher is wrong and gives you a list of excuses about why the teacher is picking on her.**

Instead of arguing with your child, schedule a conference with the teacher. Most important, tell the teacher you'd like to have Monica present at the conference, even if Monica doesn't want to go.

The fact is, including the child in the conference is the best way to sort out what's really happening between Monica and the teacher. If you don't, you're likely to go home and tell Monica what the teacher said, at which point Monica will convincingly assure you that the teacher is losing her mind, has a horrible memory, is suffering from a terminal case of PMS, or is confusing her with the *other* Monica! And round and round you'll go.

With the three of you conferring together, there's less chance for distortion, misinterpretation, or lying. A plan for solving the problem can be developed with everyone's input, and nobody (least of all you!) will get caught in the middle.

Including the child in the conference gives your youngster the healthy message that you and the teacher do communicate. It also shows that you consider school to be important and that you support the teacher's goals.

### "I'm Suspended!"

**The principal's office calls to inform you to come pick up eleven-year-old Gary, who's gotten suspended from school for his inappropriate behavior. You assure the principal that you'll do something about the problem and take your son home. On the way, you realize you have no idea what to do now . . . other than yell!**

Resist the urge to blast your son with your anger when you get him in the car to go home. This will only serve to shut off any productive communication with him about the problem. Tell him the information you were given about the situation from the school personnel, and then ask him to give his side of the story. Since schools usually do not suspend kids without good reason, you're likely to be hearing excuses rather than legitimate justifications from your child. But hear him out, anyway, just in case there's a real error on the school's part.

Although youngsters are sometimes suspended for first-time offenses, many times they've been warned before about certain inappropriate behavior and their suspension has come after a "last warning." The severity of your discipline (degree and length of restriction) will depend on consideration of these factors. But how do you deal with the child during the actual days of suspension?

Let this be a time of work, not of relaxation or fun, for your youngster. If he will be staying at home during this time, get him up at the regular hour and give him a list of chores you want him to do (clean out a closet or some cabinets; remove all your books from the shelves, dust them and put them back; thoroughly clean his room, including the woodwork; etc.). In other words, keep him busy. And, of course, no going out to play, even after school hours.

If you are taking your child to a place for child care (even his grandmother's house), make sure the person in charge of him will insist that he occupy his time, as much as it's practical to do so, in constructive activity rather than in socialization or play. He might work on school assignments, or you could give him some "assignment" (reading something and then writing a report on it for you). This same tactic would also be appropriate if you take your child to work with you.

Whether or not you continue to restrict your youngster after the suspension is over will depend on the seriousness of the infraction. If you do decide to set a further restriction involving more than a week, be sure to give him opportunities to "earn back" some privilege before the total restriction ends in order to keep him operating in a positive mode.

# CHAPTER 6

## *Sex*

If there's one topic you might feel squeamish about discussing with your child, it's likely to be sex. If you're like many parents today, you might not have grown up in an atmosphere of frank and open talk about sexual matters. Consequently, you probably don't have good built-in responses for handling this aspect of parenting. Now here you are, with your child being bombarded daily in the media about sexual topics that never even came up when you were young.

Sexuality can also bring out your parental anxieties because you know how important it will be to your child's personal development. And let's face it, sex is a complicated subject. You not only want to convey the facts and give your youngster a healthy outlook on sex, but you also want your child to develop a value system that places sex in the context of love and commitment.

Just in case you think you might not have to worry about all this until your child nears the age of puberty, prepare yourself for a shock: Questions about and situations involving sexual matters will begin to surface in toddlerhood! So let's look at some of those situations involving sex that might make you feel "on the spot" with your child.

### The Public Masturbator

**You and a couple of neighbors are sitting in the backyard watching your three-year-olds wading in your plastic kiddie pool. Suddenly, you notice that your daughter, Brandy, is standing quietly in the pool with one finger firmly lodged in her vagina!**

Just because you know intellectually that it's normal for children to touch their genitals, that doesn't mean your gut isn't going to react (probably with horror!) when you're actually confronted with your child's doing it. And you never dreamed it would happen in public! Now here you are having to do something about this situation (you can't just sit there and watch her play with herself) while worrying that your friends may be shocked and judgmental of you.

When a child is touching her genitals or masturbating in front of other people, the simplest action to take immediately is to divert her attention. You might hand her something or, if nothing is available, take her by the hand and lead her to another activity or another place. You'll save your chat about masturbation for a time when you two are alone.

When that time arrives, let your child know that all boys and girls have good feelings when they touch themselves between their legs, but that this should be done only when they are alone (perhaps in bed or in the bathroom). It's simply not okay to do this kind of touching when other grown-ups or children are around. If she asks "Why?" explain the concept of privacy by saying something like "Touching yourself that way is a very personal thing and needs to be done in private."

As for dealing with your friends in the backyard you have two options. One is to simply ignore what has occurred. The other might be to confess your mixed feelings about what just happened. Your friends might even recount how they deal with it when they find their children masturbating. You might find you can all laugh a little by exploring your mutual anxieties about this unsettling behavior.

### "What's Wrong with That Word?"

**Five-year-old Reagan is playing with a puzzle when the dog playfully grabs one of the wooden pieces and runs off with it. To your utter shock, you hear Reagan exclaim "Oh fuck!"**

Try not to act too rattled as you ask Reagan where she heard that word. After her explanation, tell her that "fuck" is an example of foul language and that you don't want her to use it. Let her know that kids get into trouble for using that word, and that the parents of her friends might not even allow her to come to their house to play if they heard her use it. Ask her if she knows what the word means, and, if she doesn't, tell her that it's a foul word for making love.

When your youngster uses any type of foul language, including cursing, you'll want to remain matter-of-fact so that you don't inadvertently give her the power to get you upset by using such words in the future. If she continues in spite of your telling her not to, you could reinforce your intentions by giving her a time-out for using inappropriate language.

Typically, your child might tell you that she heard the word at her preschool or day care, or from children in the neighborhood. However, it's not unusual for a child to be modeling her language after an older brother or sister (or even one of her parents!). This is why it's important to find out the source of her vocabulary development so you can take appropriate measures to correct the situation.

If your youngster seems to be trying to shock you by using inappropriate words, you might try a different approach. The next time she says a forbidden word, ask her to sit down with you and bring a pencil and paper. Tell her something like "You know, Reagan, I know you know some foul words. Let's see how many of them you know, okay?" Begin writing a list of the inappropriate words as your youngster dictates them, checking to make sure that she knows the meaning of each one as you write it. Then remind her of some others you've heard her say ("Didn't I hear you call your brother a 'poo-poo-head' the other day?"). Notice that many of these words will have to do with bathroom functions as well as sexual ones.

When you and your child can think of no more words for the list, count them up and exclaim, "Gosh, Reagan, you know *eleven* foul words. Wow! I didn't know a lot of those words until I was much older than you are!" What you've done, of course, is to take all the shock value your child was getting out of those forbidden words.

At that point, reinforce your statements about your not wanting her to use the words on the list as part of conversation. Let her know that you'll give her a negative consequence to remind her of this if she chooses to use one in the future. However, if she wants to say these words to herself in her room, that's fine as long as she's not saying them loud enough for others in the house to hear her.

Families differ widely regarding standards of appropriate language in the home. If your family commonly uses some words that would not be accepted in the schoolroom (or at some other homes), make this fact clear to your child.

As your youngster gets older, she might tell you (accurately) that her peers all use certain words that you consider to be inappropriate. Admit to her that there probably are different standards of language when kids talk among themselves or on the playground, but that if she chooses to use these words she's taking the chance that a grown-up will hear her (and probably think less of her).

### The Nude Dude

**You glance out the window to check on seven-year-old Derrick, who's playing in the sprinkler in the front yard. To your surprise, he's jumping through the water stark naked!**

Call Derrick to come into the house and put on a swimsuit. Let him know that it's not appropriate to be naked in public.

What you tell your child about nudity in the house will vary greatly, depending upon your own personal views. Some families are very open about it; others confine it to the bedroom or bathroom.

A happy balance that suits most families is the policy whereby parents cover up, especially around opposite-sex children, but don't make an issue of being seen nude. If their children walk in on them when they are undressed, they act naturally but move to put on a robe or underwear.

Even if you are very comfortable being nude around the house, realize that children do have sexual fantasies, long before they reach puberty. Sometimes their sexual awareness of their parents creates anxiety which produces other kinds of emotional symptoms, yet children are very unlikely to tell their parents about their fantasies (even if they are consciously aware of having them). For this reason, most child-rearing experts recommend that, at least in our society, youngsters not be exposed to excessive parental nudity.

### "Can I See?"

**You and six-year-old Annie are diapering Baby Brother and talking about how a girl's body is different from a boy's. When you tell her that every girl and woman has a vagina, she asks, "Can I see yours, Mommy?"**

Tell Annie that you'll be glad to show her a drawing in a book that shows a vagina, but that it's inappropriate for you to show her yours. However, she could get a mirror and look at her own.

Explain that a person's private parts are just that—private—and that a child should not show them to other people (except to a doctor who needs to look at them or to a parent who needs to apply medication). Reassure her that all boys and girls are very curious about how both girls' and boys' private parts look, but that they should get this information through books or by asking questions of a responsible grown-up.

While some very liberal parents might think that there's no harm in a mother revealing her genitals to her daughter (after all, boys without any effort get to see their father's genitals), most experts feel that such a situation is not only anxiety producing for the child (and for most parents) but runs the risk of seeming seductive as well.

### "But I Want to Be a Girl!"

**You're looking for four-year-old Damon and finally locate him in your bedroom. He's made one of your long silk blouses into a dress, is wearing a ton of your jewelry, and is in the process of trying to put on lipstick! When you ask him what he's doing, he tells you that he wants to be a girl.**

Even though you've read books that say it's perfectly normal for little boys and girls to play "dress up" in clothes of the opposite sex, seeing this behavior—and then having your son state that he wants to be a girl—can be quite upsetting. "Oh my God! Does my son *really* want to be a girl?" might be your unspoken thought.

Realize that it's a common occurrence for preschool youngsters of both sexes to experiment with dressing up in the opposite sex's clothing and to say they'd like to be the opposite sex. They are just experimenting with different roles, much as they might pretend to be an animal or a movie character. If you don't make a big deal about it, chances are your child's interest in this type of play will soon pass, or will crop up only occasionally.

Ask Damon why he thinks it would be so wonderful to be a girl. When he's finished telling you, you might want to point out some of the advantages of being a boy. And let him know that people are born boys and girls—and that's the way they stay (no need to get into the issue of sex change operations with a young child).

Let Damon know that if he likes putting on costumes, you'll provide a box for him with old clothes and accessories for him to use. If he asks for women's garments and accessories, go ahead and provide them. Of course, you'll also want to stock it with items that are suitable to boys (caps, Dad's shirts and pants, coats, ties, etc.).

If your son seems to get more fascinated with wearing women's clothing and/or steadily maintains that he wants to be a girl, you might begin letting him know that you'd prefer him to dress as a male by saying something like "Let's see you in some boy clothes, Damon. You're a boy and I'd much rather see you dress like a boy." This mild discouragement tactic will usually solve the problem.

You might also want to begin talking with your son about why he sometimes thinks he'd rather be a girl. It may be that he wants to take gymnastics, but thinks it's only a girls' activity. Or he might be worried about about his schoolwork and is envious that the girls in his class seem to have an easier time with academics. Giving him information that both sexes can participate in all types of recreational or sports activities and/or finding out about his anxieties and giving him appropriate reassurance might eliminate his feelings about wishing to be a girl.

Before you start jumping to conclusions about the possibility of your child's having a potential gender-identification problem, remember to stop and ask yourself some commonsense questions. Does he steadily maintain over a period of time that he wants to be a girl? Does he continue dressing in female clothing in spite of your discouraging it? Does he "sneak" this type of dressing, acting guilty when you happen to catch him? If your answer is yes to any of these questions, you'll want to consult a mental health professional for further evaluation of the complicated sexual identification issue.

## "But It's Only a Magazine!"

**You have the day off from work and decide to do the laundry before the weekend. As you're changing the sheets on nine-year-old Keith's bed, you find a copy of *Playboy* stuffed between the mattress and the box spring!**

Obviously, your method of handling this with your youngster is going to depend on your own attitude about this kind of magazine. And if you or your mate subscribe to it, you'll be treating the situation differently than if you would never allow such reading material in your home.

When you have an opportunity, confront Keith with the fact that you found the magazine. Ask him where he got it, if you don't already know. You'll want to remain fairly matter-of-fact about the magazine in order not to make it any more enticing than it already is to your child.

One approach might be for Mom or Dad to sit down with Keith and look at the magazine with him. This tactic takes away the thrill of feeling secretive about looking at such material and makes his seeing it less powerful. Acknowledge that all boys and girls are curious about what the opposite sex looks like naked, and about how people look when they are involved in sexual activity. Point out that the sexually oriented pictures, however, can be interpreted as very demeaning to women and men. They may give the false impression that women just exist for the sexual pleasure of men, and that men are sexual machines, not people with feelings. You might also mention that most people don't have bodies that look just like those of the models in the pictures.

If you do allow your youngster to keep the magazine, let him know that you'll take it away if you find that he's showing it to a young brother or sister or passing it around the neighborhood. Tell him that many parents would not look kindly on a youngster who introduced their children to this form of reading.

Another approach might be simply to ask Keith to give you the magazine and tell him that you don't allow such material in the house (assuming the magazine came from a source outside your home). Let him know that his curiosity about the magazine is very normal, but that you don't approve of his viewing it.

What if you have a subscription to this type of magazine, but you still don't want your child reading it? Tell him that you don't consider this reading material to be suitable for a child his age, and let him know how old he'll have to be before you'll give him your approval to read it.

Even if you decide to be liberal about the magazine your child was reading, you might not feel so tolerant of magazines that show hard-core pornography. If you find your child with such material, tell him you don't approve of it and take it away from him. You might also want to let him know that these pictures usually do not show sex in the context of deep love and commitment.

The fact is that, whether or not you like it, almost every child is exposed sooner or later to sexually oriented literature. By treating it matter-of-factly and telling your youngster what you think about it, you help him put it in a healthy perspective.

### "We're Playing Doctor!"

**Seven-year-old Dorothy and six-year-old Roy, a neighbor, are playing with Dorothy's new dollhouse in her room. When you take a snack to them, you see that the door to Dorothy's room is closed. Opening it, you're shocked to see the two of them on the bed without clothes and playing doctor!**

Immediately tell both children to put on their clothes, staying in the room while they dress, and then tell them to come to the kitchen for their snack. Sit down with them and calmly tell them that they must keep their clothes on when they play.

Explain that everybody has private parts of his or her body, and that it's not okay to look at or touch someone else's private parts. Be sure to reassure them that it's perfectly normal to be curious about what these private body parts look like, but that they should ask a parent to show them a book with drawings or pictures that will answer their questions rather than to explore each other's bodies.

If the children were involved in specific sexual activity, you should ask them where they got the idea for it. Have they seen someone else doing this? Has someone done this to them before? Did they see this on TV? In other words, check to find out why your child is involved in precocious sexual behavior since such activity *may* indicate that a youngster has been sexually abused.

However, children participating in specific sex acts is far less common than simply undressing and playing doctor.

To prevent a recurrence of her inappropriate looking, touching, and so on, instruct your child to leave the doors open when she has company in her room (even if the company is a child of the same sex). Also, tell the parents of the other child what happened. They can reinforce the message of "no sex play" to their child and also check out if there's been any sexual abuse to him. But be sure you let them know that you're aware that sex play among children is very common, even expected, and that you're certainly not accusing their child of being a monster.

### The Inappropriate Toucher

**Six-year-old Mac is sitting between you and a friend on the sofa, watching television and eating popcorn. Being newly fascinated with women's bodies, Mac suddenly reaches over and touches your friend's breast.**

Remove the child's hand if it's still touching the breast and say something like "Mac, it's not polite to touch a lady's breast. That's a private part of her body, honey." A quick meaningful "I'm sorry" to your friend is all that should be necessary.

Later, when you and your child are alone, go into more detail about everyone having private parts of his or her body. An occasion such as this gives you another opportunity to discuss the whole matter of inappropriate touching, *and* to let your child know that he should always tell you if anyone touches him inappropriately.

If your child persists in this behavior in spite of your explanation, reinforce your disapproval by giving him a negative consequence (removing a privilege). Let him know that his actions are aggressive, and not at all funny, and that they violate the other person's right to have his or her body respected.

### "What Are You and Daddy Doing?"

**You and your mate are in bed making love, totally uncovered. All of a sudden, you become aware that eight-year-old Mandy has opened the bedroom door and is standing there watching you!**

Get out of bed, slip something on, and take Mandy back to her bed. Tell her, with as much calm as you can muster, something like "Daddy and I were making love, honey. I'll talk with you more about it in the morning."

The next day, remind Mandy of the incident the night before, even if she doesn't bring it up (you want the opportunity to correct any misinterpretations). Without making her defensive, casually find out what she saw when she came into the room, how she felt about it, and whether she has any questions she'd like to ask. If she seems shy or embarrassed, let her know that it's perfectly fine for her to ask questions, and that she's done nothing wrong. The more casual you can be about the whole matter, the more your child will be able to feel comfortable with this conversation.

Realize that youngsters who have witnessed sexual activity or heard it often misinterpret sounds of passion as "somebody's getting hurt!" Therefore, you'll want to tell your child that making love is a very special and pleasurable way a man and woman show love for one another. Tell her directly that making love doesn't hurt, but feels very nice.

If your child asks specific questions about sexual intercourse, or about any sexual activity she has witnessed, answer her questions matter-of-factly with a behavioral description ("the man puts his penis into the woman's vagina") of these activities. If she has a negative reaction to anything you tell her ("That's gross!"), reassure her that you felt the same way at her age, but that as she gets older and understands sex better, she'll probably change her mind. Let her know that you realize that she'll have many questions about sex as she gets older, and that you and she will be discussing it many times before she's grown up.

You might also take this opportunity to remind your youngster that she should always knock on a closed bedroom or bathroom door and get permission to enter the room. People close their doors for privacy, and their wishes should be respected.

# CHAPTER 7

## *Fears and Anxieties*

Even in the happiest of childhoods, kids develop fears and anxieties that are often beyond a parent's control. And let's face it, some kids are more sensitive than others. They become upset easily and worry more than their more confident counterparts.

Obviously a traumatic event can increase a youngster's insecurities. Yet many children's fears typically occur without the presence of any external trauma. In fact, some (fear of monsters, nightmares) are so common that parents almost know to expect them.

When children are afraid, they usually need two things: information and reassurance. They also will be less likely to become frightened in the first place if they are told what to expect (rehearsing fire drills, a visit to the hospital before admission, and so on). Many parents, in an effort to protect their youngsters from worry, will try to shield them from any truth that might be upsetting (Mom has a serious illness, the child will need a shot when she goes to the doctor, and so on). However, kids can deal with "truth" far more easily than with uncertainty.

Let's look at some of the common childhood insecurities that can easily put a parent "on the spot."

### "But I Saw a Monster!"

**Five-year-old Arnie, whom you tucked into bed a half hour ago, comes running into the family room yelling, "Daddy, there's a monster under my bed!"**

Gather Arnie into your arms and quietly tell him, "Honey, there are no monsters. You're perfectly safe." As he settles down, explain to him that there are play monsters like the ones he sees on television, but there are no *real* monsters. You might also tell him that there are people who dress up in monster suits on television or in the movies, where the cameras have made a picture of a bug seem much bigger to make it look like a scary monster. Certainly, a wise parent will monitor television viewing carefully (especially for children up through age six or seven) for "scary" content.

Sometimes parents unwittingly scare their kids more by making statements like "Well with the dogs outside and all our doors locked, the monsters couldn't possibly get in." What a child really needs to hear is the simple truth that there are no monsters.

Take the child back into his room and reassure him that there's nothing under the bed, in the closet, behind the drapes, and so on. Encourage him to look for himself, but if he won't, go ahead and go through the motions for him. This extra act on your part should dispel any lingering doubts. Leave a night light on in his room for extra comfort if he wants it.

(If your child persists in worrying about monsters, read about nightmares in the next section for an explanation about the psychological dynamics behind both nightmares and the persistent fear of monsters.)

### The Night Screamer

**You're awakened in the middle of the night by four-year-old Sean's screams. You rush into his bedroom to find him in bed crying hysterically, sweating, and pulling on his pajamas or picking at his face or body. You try to comfort him, but he doesn't seem to hear anything you say. When he does awaken he has no memory of what happened.**

Simply comfort Sean when he awakens and say something like "I love you, sweetie. Go back to sleep." He's probably had a "night terror," which differs from a nightmare. The child who has a nightmare is either awake when you reach him or he will quickly wake up when you talk to him. He'll listen to reason and calm down fairly quickly. He might even be able to tell you what the nightmare was about. The child who has had a night terror will probably have no memory of what happened and is likely to be surprised to see you in his room. This is why it's best just to tell him good-night and not to mention what happened since describing the event could frighten him.

Occasional night terrors are common in young children but can appear up to early adolescence. Their cause is not known, although many experts feel that stress increases their frequency. Interestingly, they are not related to the REM (rapid eye movement) stage of sleep that is associated with dream activity, as nightmares are. Physiologically the child is thought to be in a half-sleep–half-awake state, and the signs of anxiety that frighten parents (screams, sweating, rapid heartbeat, mumbling, pulling at clothes or the body) totally disappear when the child wakes up. There is no cause for concern unless a child gets out of bed and walks around during the episode, in which case he needs to be evaluated by a pediatric neurologist to rule out possible seizures. Night terrors typically last from five to fifteen minutes and usually occur during the first four hours after the child falls asleep. Nightmares usually occur after the youngster has been asleep for at least four hours.

The point to remember is that even if your child is yelling, screaming, and having other signs of distress, he cannot help what he's doing. He's not trying to "manipulate" you or to "get attention." He simply can't control what he's doing and in fact has no memory of it.

If your child wakens you because of a nightmare, reassure him that he's only had a bad dream—that what happened in the nightmare really didn't happen at all. Tell him that something might be bothering him and that's why he had a scary dream. Encourage him to tell you about the nightmare if he wants to, but don't force it. Talking about the content and telling himself out loud that he was only dreaming will sometimes help a child work through his fear. Forcing him to talk about the dream, however, can frighten him more by making the whole thing seem too important.

Teach your youngster how he can comfort himself when he has had a nightmare (so that, in time, he will not need to waken you). One way to do this is to help him think of soothing things he can say to himself after he wakes up. For example, instead of telling himself, "Gosh, what if there really *is* a giant purple lizard running after me with a knife to kill me!" he could say, "That was a dream. There really is no such thing as a giant purple lizard. It's safe to go back to sleep." Then he probably will be able to fall asleep quickly.

Tell your child that he can remind himself that you are right down the hall and that you've made the house safe by locking all doors and windows. You might also pick out one of his stuffed animals or dolls and tell him to cuddle with it to remind himself that he's safe.

A youngster who is having frequent nightmares, or is persistently worrying about monsters, is often afraid, probably unconsciously, that he's done something wrong. It might be that he really did do something he knows he shouldn't have, or it might be that he's only *thought* about doing it. Feeling that he's been bad in some way, he expects to be punished. What better way to be punished than to imagine something or someone ominously chasing after him?

You can sometimes help your child by sharing this information with him. Encourage him to tell you if he's done something wrong.

If he has, thank him for telling you, discuss the situation and consequences, and then let him know that everyone makes mistakes. Teach him to forgive himself when he goofs and to learn from the mistake.

Be sure to reassure him that "thoughts" about doing wrong things are not the same as actually doing those things and that all children have such thoughts. Let him know that it's perfectly normal to feel angry even at people he loves very much, and that those angry feelings and thoughts don't mean he's a bad person or that something bad is going to happen to him.

### "But I Didn't Make 100!"

**Eight-year-old Alysha comes home from school with a hint of tears in her eyes. When you ask her to tell you what's wrong, she bursts into tears, pulls a test out of her notebook, and hands it to you. To your amazement you see that she scored a 93!**

You might say something like "Honey, that's a very high score. Why on earth are you upset about a ninety-three?" but know that with Alysha's perfectionistic tendencies, this comment will only scratch the surface of the issue. She'll probably insist that she should have made 100.

Of course, you'll want to help your child be not so hard on herself. Tell her that it's unrealistic to expect to make 100 consistently or to do anything *perfectly*, for that matter. Let her know that everyone makes mistakes and that mistakes actually help a person learn. If a person learns from her mistakes, she doesn't have to make the same one again.

But talking about all of this is just the first step. The other involves asking yourself if you or your mate are somehow (in spite of your words to the contrary) giving your youngster a message that she *has* to be perfect.

For example, many parents, usually without realizing it, rarely accept what a child does as "enough." It is as if these parents have the philosophy that if a child is to grow up to be a successful, productive citizen, a parent's job is to let the child know every possible way she could improve on anything she does ("Honey, thank you for making the bed. But there's a little wrinkle under the pillow on the left side!").

What this parenting approach really teaches is that nothing a youngster does is quite good enough. A child might rebel and not even try, since she thinks she could never do anything right. Or she might internalize the parent's value system and become a perfectionist.

Another way a youngster might learn perfectionism is through a parent's example. Even though she might be *told* not to worry about being perfect, she sees her mom or dad getting uptight if everything isn't "just right." If you are a parent with these tendencies, try poking fun at yourself when you get into a perfectionistic mode. Point it out when you make little mistakes and laugh about them with your child. The message that a person doesn't have to be perfect will come through much louder than any words you could say.

### The Midnight Intruder

**It's 3:00 A.M. and your sound sleep is interrupted when six-year-old Cody climbs into your bed. You know from experience that if you take him back to his bed he'll sob that he's scared and then cry for a long time. But you know he needs to learn to sleep in his own bed (and you're getting sick of losing sleep every night!).**

Let him sleep with you *one* more night, but be determined to implement a new system tomorrow. The longer you allow him to sleep in your bed, the harder the habit will be to break.

The next day, talk with Cody about his habit of coming into your bed in the middle of the night. Tell him the truth: that you get angry when he disturbs your sleep (unless it's an emergency, which you need to define for him) and that he needs to be a "big boy" and stay in his own bed all night. Tell him that you know he's scared when he wakes up but that he must learn to be brave (which is better than telling him he shouldn't be scared).

Then ask your child to help think of some ways he could help himself not to be so scared if he wakes up during the night. Would he feel more comfortable if his room were rearranged (his bed closer to his parents' room, away from a window, and so on)? Is there a special stuffed animal or doll that he could sleep with to remind himself that he's safe? Would it help to have a radio playing softly or to have a light turned on? Would he like to have some "memento" to remind himself that his parents are nearby (a picture on the dresser, one of Mom's or Dad's T-shirts to wear to bed or keep nearby)? Would he like the family pet to sleep in his room (if this is allowed)?

Be sure to let your child know about the safety features in your house such as a burglar alarm, locks on doors and windows, and so on. Tell him that you've made the house as safe as you possibly can and that you are also close by when he's alseep.

After settling on any ideas your child has for helping himself to feel more comfortable, break the news to him that the new program will start *that night.* Let him know that you expect him to handle this and not to disturb you. For a little extra incentive you might let him earn a treat or privilege in the mornings after he's remained in his bed all night.

After this preparation, gear up to go through the hassle of putting your youngster back in his bed immediately should he come into your room in the night. You'll have to be consistent if you want to break the habit. After you talk with him and with the promise of an incentive, you might be lucky enough not to have much of a battle.

If you find yourself resisting these suggestions, it might be that a part of you really likes the idea of having your child in bed with you. If this is the case, let him know that he can come into bed in the mornings—but *after* a certain time on the clock. This plan allows your youngster to learn to sleep by himself, prevents you from losing sleep, and also lets you and your child have some special cuddling time in bed.

### "I Want to Marry Daddy!"

**Normally well-behaved Jenna, age five, won't let you and your mate have a moment's peace when she's with the two of you. She often interrupts your conversations, and when you and your mate are sitting close together she insists that she sit between you. Now, as your mate gives you a kiss on the forehead, Jenna announces that you cannot kiss each other.**

Tell Jenna, "No, honey, Daddy and I love each other. Of course we're going to kiss when we feel like it." Then decide to have a chat with Jenna at the first opportunity.

Realize that a child may become jealous of her parent's relationship. This situation can occur if the youngster is not getting much of either parent's time and might represent a cry for more attention. Or the child's behavior might result from one or both parents' giving the youngster the feeling that the child is the most important person in the family. In this case, the youngster simply expects to be the center of attention at all times.

Often a child will become rivalrous with the parent of the same sex; for example a girl will be jealous of her mother because the child wants to be her daddy's favorite. Such rivalry is most likely to surface when a youngster is four or five years old, since children in this stage often have fantasies of wanting to be married to the parent of the opposite sex. They sense a special relationship between their parents, and want to be the favored one instead of the parent of the same sex. If this situation occurs, a child needs to be given the message that Daddy and Mommy have a special relationship, but that the child can find a man and woman *like* Daddy or Mommy to have a special relationship with when that child grows up.

Begin talking with your child about her jealous behavior by pointing out that it's important for her not to interrupt other people when they are talking. Let her know that you're going to remind her of this fact if she interrupts your conversation in the future.

Next, tell her that sometimes you and your mate want to talk about something that is "grown-up talk." Although she might be in the room you'll expect her to play quietly rather than participating in the conversation. Also explain that sometimes you and your mate want to sit next to each other on the couch. At those times you expect her not to climb in between you unless she's invited to do so. Let your youngster know that hugs and kisses are normal expressions of affection between a husband and wife and that you have no intention of stopping them.

Of course you'll want to reassure your child that your relationship with your partner has nothing to do with your love for her. Tell her that there are many different kinds of love and that your love for her is always there even if you are also spending time or being affectionate with someone else.

You might think it's a little hard-nosed to follow through and insist that your child respect your wishes about this. After all, you and your mate could limit your talking and being affectionate together to those times when your child isn't around. The problem with this solution is that it gives your child an inappropriate sense of control and can also contribute to her fantasies that she can have one of you "all to herself." In the long run your youngster will be better off knowing that her parents do have a special relationship of their own apart from being her parents.

## "Who Do You Love the Most?"

**During a birthday party for seven-year-old Stacy, you notice that her nine-year-old sister, Shannon, has been unusually quiet. After the party you ask Shannon if something is bothering her. She replies, "Mommy, who do you love the most, Stacy or me?"**

Before you say, "I love both of you the same," ask yourself how this answer would feel to you if you were in Shannon's position. Probably not too comforting. "Just the same" smacks of a cop-out.

Instead, say something like "Honey, you are my Shannon, and

there's no one else like you in the whole wide world. You are very smart, very thoughtful of other people, and you really know how to make me laugh. I couldn't possibly compare you and Stacy because there's no other Stacy in the world either. I love you both with all my heart, so there's no possible way to compare my love for each of you." This type of answer makes a child feel loved uniquely and makes it clear that the question of loving one youngster more than another is unanswerable.

After making it clear that you can't compare amounts of love, discuss the context in which you think your child came up with this question. In this case, you'd discuss her feelings about her sister's birthday party. Let her know that it's very hard to watch someone else gets lots of gifts while she gets none and that her jealous feelings are quite natural. Then remind her that her turn will come when she too will experience being in the limelight and receiving lots of goodies.

### "But That's Not Fair!"

**At the mall earlier in the day, you spotted a marvelous sale at a children's shop and picked up a bargain swimsuit for seven-year-old Tricia. Eleven-year-old Becky is furious that you didn't bring her a surprise. "That's not fair!" she screams as she runs off to her room.**

When Becky has calmed down, have a talk with her about fairness. Explain that "fair" doesn't always mean "even." Let her know that there are times when a parent gives something to one child and not to another because of circumstances. In this case, a swimsuit that fit her sister was on sale. If there had been a swimsuit on sale in the preteen sizes, Becky would have been the one getting it rather than her sister.

Point out other circumstances when a parent might do something for one child and not for another. For instance, if a child is sick, she's likely to need more attention than one who's well. Or a youngster might be having some immediate problem (struggling with a school assignment, grieving over her pet guinea pig that just died) that requires a parent to give priority for a while to her needs over those of other family members.

Remember that children's unreasonable complaints about being treated unfairly compared to their siblings reflect their insecurities about being loved. You'll need to explain that what is "fair" is that a parent meet the needs of each child whenever needs appear, not that a parent has to spend the same amount of time or money on each child on every occasion.

### "But You Wouldn't Let Me Have That When I Was That Age!"

**Eleven-year-old Marianne is livid. You just bought her nine-year-old sister a pair of designer jeans, but you wouldn't let Marianne have any designer items until she got to sixth grade!**

Let Marianne know that this is a typical "older sibling" complaint. Many times younger brothers and sisters get to do or have something at a younger age than when the oldest child was allowed to do or have it.

What happens is that times and circumstances change. Parents tend to "hold out" longer on certain privileges (spending the night at a friend's, having designer clothes, going shopping without adult supervision, dating) with their oldest child. Parents are more likely to ease up a little with younger children after having been through these kinds of situations with their older youngsters. This pattern just seems to be a fact of parental human nature.

Or perhaps when Marianne was eight years old, the family budget wouldn't accommodate buying designer jeans. Parents often have more money to spend (Mom and/or Dad get a promotion) as their children get older, so younger children reap the benefits of a more affluent budget.

Of course, an older child also gets the benefits of a higher family income. Point out to your older child that you might *now* spend twice the amount on her school clothes than you would have spent several years ago, not because of her age, but because of your increased budget.

Your explanation is not likely to make your child jump for joy, but it may give her a better understanding of this age-old phenomenon of younger siblings getting privileges at earlier ages. Remember that her worrying about this is just another manifestation of her underlying concern that she is loved as much as her sibling.

### "No, I'm Not Sick!"

**Seven-year-old Abe is unusually quiet as he gets ready for school. He denies that anything is wrong, so you attribute his lack of usual zest to his getting to bed a little later the night before. A few hours later, the school calls to tell you that Abe is vomiting and running a fever. When you question your son on the way home from school, he admits that he'd been feeling terrible since he got out of bed!**

When Abe is feeling well enough to talk, ask him to tell you why he denied feeling ill earlier that morning. Was he afraid you'd be angry at him? Does he think illness is a punishment for something he did, or thought, that he considers wrong?

You might wonder why your child would even think such erroneous thoughts, but ask yourself what messages you might have given him about illness. If he gets a cold, are the first words out of your mouth "Well didn't I tell you to put on a coat yesterday when it was chilly?" or "Have you been taking your jacket off on the way to school even though I've told you a hundred times not to?" In other words, the *way* you query your child about what might have led up to his illness can leave him with the impression that you blame him for getting sick.

Sometimes even when you've said nothing to leave such an impression, children will fantasize that illness is related to wrongdoing. After all, why would something bad happen to them unless they deserved it? Explain to your child that people become sick from many different causes, but never because they are bad or have done something wrong. Illness is a way for the body to give a person a signal that something is wrong with his body, not his behavior.

Some children, especially those who have been subjected to uncomfortable medical procedures, will not admit that they are feeling sick because they fear having to go to the doctor, taking medicine that tastes yucky, or having to stay in bed. In this case, sympathize with your child's understandable reluctance to go to the doctor, but reassure him that such treatment is the fastest way to help himself get well.

### "I Have Bad Thoughts!"

**Nine-year-old Karen has been looking worried and upset the past few days. After you've made several attempts to get her to talk to you about this she confesses that she's having "bad thoughts." Further inquiry reveals that she's been angry with her brother and wished he'd have an accident on his bike.**

Karen needs a lot of reassurance that angry thoughts are not "bad" and that all children sometimes have such thoughts toward members of their family and other people they love. Explain to her that if her brother really did have a wreck on his bike, she'd feel very sorry for him. It's just that when a person is angry she might wish that something bad would happen to the person she's angry with, but it doesn't mean she'd *really* want the wish to come true.

It's also important that your child understands that angry thoughts do not *cause* bad things to happen to people. For example, if her brother did have a wreck on his bike it would not be *because* she'd had the earlier thought about it when she was angry at him. Angry thoughts are just thoughts; they don't cause events to happen.

Sometimes youngsters will think they are having "bad thoughts" when they think about sexual matters or if they are feeling guilty about masturbation. If this is true of your child, reassure her that all children think about sex and all children think about or enjoy touching their private parts. Such thoughts or actions do not mean that a child is "bad" or that something is wrong with her.

If a child becomes preoccupied with her "bad thoughts" despite your giving her reassurance, professional consultation is recommended.

### THE DREAMER

**Ten-year-old Dana is crushed because she didn't get moved up into the "intermediate" ballet class at her dancing school. You are not at all surprised, however, because Dana is rather awkward and doesn't have any talent for dancing. Yet since she was six she's wanted to be a ballerina more than anything in the world.**

First, express your sympathy for Dana's not getting moved up to the intermediate class by saying something like "Honey, I know you're very disappointed. I'm so sorry it didn't work out the way you wanted."

Next talk to Dana about what it takes to get to a goal, in this case to become a ballerina. True, it takes hard work and practice, but point out that talent also plays a part in how quickly a person will progress. Some people move their bodies like dancers, others have to work very hard to master this skill, and some never quite attain the mastery they desire. Let her know that maybe she's not a "natural-born dancer," that she's someone who will have to work very hard to accomplish becoming a ballerina. Ask her if she's really willing to put that much effort into it or whether, perhaps, she'd rather pursue something she has more natural talent for (art, music, creative writing, and so on).

Your goal is not to tell her you don't think she'll ever make it as a ballerina, because there are many people who've been determined enough to accomplish feats that others never thought they'd attain. Even if you are correct in your assessment, let your child learn gradually that she's not well suited for dancing as you also encourage her in other pursuits.

In other words, don't give your child false hope, but don't dampen her spirit or her self-esteem. If she is truly unsuited for dancing she'll become more aware of this fact as she matures. Instead, give her a realistic picture of the hurdles she'll need to surmount, help her keep her options open by pointing out other activities she's good at, and let nature take its course.

### The Curious Adoptee

**You're tucking nine-year-old Zac into bed for the night when out of the blue he says, "Mom, why didn't my birth mother want me?"**

From the day you adopted Zac, you knew that this question might come up, but that doesn't make it any easier to answer him. First ask Zac what ideas he's already had about why his birth mother gave him up for adoption. Is he picturing her as some famous or saintly person who had to sacrifice giving up her child for a higher cause? Is he thinking his mother was some kind of criminal? Is he thinking that she had lots of children and just had to give one away? Finding out Zac's fantasies about this situation can help you gear your answer to meet his specific needs.

If you know the circumstances of the birth mother's decision to give up her child, tell them to your child in a positive way. If negative information is involved (the mother was a prostitute, in prison, and so on), describe the birth mother as "troubled" or having "emotional problems" that prevented her from being able to keep a child. If you do not know the birth mother's circumstances, tell your child this fact.

Whether you do or don't know specific information about the birth mother, help your child see that a mother's giving up her baby for adoption is motivated by love for the child and a desire that the baby have a better life than the mother could offer. Let your child know that this decision must have been very difficult for the birth mother, but that she put his welfare above her own wishes to keep him.

Many adopted youngsters have the fantasy that they did something wrong that caused their birth mothers to give them away, so you'll need to tell your child directly that this is not so. This is especially likely to crop up if your child is having problems in school or at home. He might jump to the conclusion that his birth mother magically knew he'd have such problems and decided to give him away because she didn't want to deal with such difficulties. Because he's feeling bad about himself, the whole issue of a birth mother's giving him away comes to the surface. So reassure your youngster that birth mothers don't give their children up for adoption because of anything to do with the child (or the child's personality).

### "I Won't Stay Here Without You!"

**You take eight-year-old Grady to his first baseball practice, delighted that he wants to be on the church team. You know he's a little shy and you think a team sport will help him gain a sense of independence. As the coach calls the roll and you get ready to leave the park, Grady comes running up frantically, grabs your arm, and says, "Mom, I'm not staying unless you stay with me!"**

Since this is the first practice, go ahead and stay. Realize that your child might need this extra boost until he has some familiarity with the coach, the other kids, the rules of the game, and so on.

Make it clear on the way home, however, that you won't be able to stay for every practice (even if you could). Let him know that you realize he'd prefer for you to stay but that you have other things you need to do during most of his practices. Tell him that he'll soon feel more comfortable as he gets used to his coach and teammates, and that he'll also feel better about himself knowing he's able to stay like the other kids without having to have a parent in attendance.

Realize that your child might have any number of fears about staying by himself at a practice. He may be worried that you won't return to pick him up, that the other kids will bully him, that he won't be able to perform as well as the other children, or that the coach will yell at him. Obviously you'll want to talk to him about his specific concerns and then give him the reassurance he needs.

If your youngster continues to balk or threatens to quit the team unless you'll stay, consider "weaning" him by staying for a part of the practice and then leaving after shorter amounts of time as each practice occurs. You might also arrange for your child to be picked up by another child's parent to get yourself out of this difficult spot.

Remember, too, that you usually have an ally in the coach, so discuss the problem with him. He might have an idea for getting your youngster to participate more readily, such as assigning him a "job" to do upon arriving at the ball field.

### "I Can't Do Anything Right!"

**You're helping eight-year-old Kenneth with his math homework and he's finally down to the last problem. He makes a minor mistake, tries to erase it, and creates a hole in the paper. Suddenly he bursts into tears and wails, "I never can do anything right!"**

Put the books and paper aside and tell Kenneth that he can finish that math problem later. Help him to calm down, perhaps by having him take some deep breaths, by making him a snack, or just by putting your arms around him.

When he's calm, talk with Kenneth about his expectations for himself. Tell him there's a big difference between making a mistake and "never being able to do anything right." But before you jump in and point out all the things he *can* do, ask him to tell you what "other things" he thinks he can't do well.

Listen carefully as he lists the things he thinks he does poorly. Are they related to academics? Social issues? Problems in the family? Once you know what's troubling him, give him some concrete suggestions for improving the situation. For example, if schoolwork is an issue, talk with the teacher to see whether some type of educational testing would be helpful. If he's having social problems, give him some ideas for handling them. If he tells you that the other parent is always mad at him, suggest that you call a family meeting to talk about his perception.

When you're through talking about "problems," ask your child to tell you some things he likes about himself. If he can't come up with anything, help him out. Obviously you'll want him to acknowledge his strengths and talents in order to bolster his sagging self-esteem.

# CHAPTER 8

## *Oppositional Behavior*

There's almost nothing that can get on a parent's nerves more than a child who's chronically balky, complaining, negative, or grumpy. No matter how much you try to please this kid, you never seem to be able to satisfy him!

The child who is oppositional sets himself up for a circular trap. The more he behaves this way, the more negative feedback he gets from the people around him. This in turn makes him angrier—and even more oppositional.

The way out of this cycle is for a parent to find a way to cut the negativity short, give it zero attention, and then reward the child with attention when he *isn't* being oppositional. Easier said than done!

Let's look at some of the "hot seat" situations that can come up for a parent when a child is being oppositional.

### THE UNCONTAINABLE SPIRIT!

**Jared, age four, does not mind well either at home or in his preschool. You've tried to use time-outs to discipline him, but he refuses to stay in the time-out room!**

First ask yourself if you're giving Jared attention when he's supposed to be in time-out. Do you talk with him awhile when he comes out of his room, or do you unceremoniously insist that he immediately go back in the room without trying to convince, encourage, explain, or threaten? Remember that even if you're angry, talking to your child at all *is* giving him attention. Kids will usually opt for negative attention rather than no attention. Obviously, you want to give your child lots of attention, but you want it to be the positive kind.

Also make it clear that when Jared comes out of his room before the time-out is over he'll need to go back in for a *longer* time period. A three-minute time-out is plenty long for a preschooler, with added increments of one minute if the time needs to be extended. Setting a timer can help both you and your child know exactly when a time-out is over and keeps you from having to answer your youngster's "Is the time up yet, Mommy?"

If you begin when your child is a toddler to discipline yourself to consistently and matter-of-factly *insist* that he stay in his room for time-out, he'll probably respond without further problems. However, if your child is very strong-willed or if you're just beginning to set limits on a youngster who's not used to being disciplined, he might refuse to stay in time-out no matter how consistently and correctly you administer it. When the previous measures haven't worked, consider adding something new to the system—a chain lock. But before you say, "What! Lock a child in his room!" read on with an open mind.

Conventional "locking a child in his room" is definitely *not* recommended. A youngster can become extremely frightened behind a closed, locked door. He can have fantasies of being abandoned, of having the house catch on fire and burning up in his room, or of hearing monsters outside the door. You certainly do not want to frighten him or to make him feel that he's not safe.

However, placing a chain lock (the kind that lets the door remain open a few inches) on the outside of a child's door, very high up so he can't unlatch it by standing on a chair, provides a very different experience for the child. He can see out of his room and know that nothing catastrophic is happening. Even if he is able to see only down a hallway, the crack in the door allows him to see and hear reality instead of letting his imagination run wild with scary thoughts.

Interestingly, if you decide to use a chain lock, you probably won't need it more than a few times. The way to use it is as follows: Tell your child that when he goes to time-out, he's free to leave his door open if he wants. If he comes out before you tell him to, however, put him back in his room with the chain lock on. The lock will remain on until the time-out is over. While your child will probably test you to see if you will really use the lock, he's unlikely to require it very often. There's just something insulting to him about having to have that chain attached!

A reminder: If you put a lock on your child's door at bedtime (to keep him from running out of his room), reassure him that you will take it off as soon as he's asleep. You don't want him to worry that he won't be able to come out of his room if he needs to during the night.

You might also worry that if you prevent your child's leaving the time-out room, he'll one-up you by kicking the door or walls or by throwing things around his room. If he kicks the door or walls, go into his room and remove his shoes and then leave him for the duration of the time-out. If he throws things around that are breakable or could damage the walls, walk into his room and remove those items, letting him know he'll have to earn them back at a later time. If he makes a mess of his room, insist that he clean it up after the time-out is over (perhaps helping him if the job is too monumental for a young child).

If you find that you're giving your child numerous time-outs in a day (after the initial testing period when you're just starting to use this technique), rethink your expectations. Perhaps you are trying to modify too many of your child's behaviors at once. Better to focus on just one, such as hitting or kicking, and then move on to others. You don't want your child to experience you as coercive or to feel that he can never please you.

Your persistence in getting your child to accept a time-out will pay off immeasurably since time-out is one of the most useful discipline methods for children up through the elementary years. Time-out establishes your control as a parent and sends the healthy message to your child that you will set limits on his inappropriate behavior. Realize that you're giving him a greater sense of security by letting him know that you can keep things in control. Children feel safe when they can count on the grown-ups to set rules and then follow through with them. Obviously, parents also need to provide a balance between necessary control and overcontrol, allowing youngsters to make age-appropriate decisions and relinquishing controls as the child matures.

## The Tuner-Outer

**Ten-year-old Christopher has been playing with his baseballs cards all morning. You've asked him four times to carry some folded towels from the family room to the bathroom cabinet and gotten a perfunctory "uh-huh" each time you've mentioned it. But he's still sitting there!**

You could walk over and gather up the baseball cards. When Christopher looks at you incredulously, simply tell him you'll allow him to have them back as soon as the towels are in the cabinet.

Kids will tell you that they know how many times a parent will tell them to do something before the parent *means* it. With some parents it's the first time; with others it's not until a parent turns red in the face. Typically a child won't act until the parent takes some action, especially when the child has learned that a parent makes threats but doesn't follow through with them.

The solution to getting your child to do something the first time you ask (within reason, of course) is simply not to keep giving him so many chances before you take action. If he wants to delay your request ("just till this program is over"), set a deadline (when the program is over) and then stick to it.

Fortunately, once your youngster has learned that he must follow through on your requests in a timely manner, he'll quit testing you. He'll know you mean what you say and act on that assumption.

If your child seems resentful of your requests, check yourself to see if you've really been *asking* him rather than *telling* him. A "would you please . . ." is good manners for parents too. It's important to respect your youngster's agenda and feelings: In this case, "I see you're busy now, Christopher, but I'd like these towels put away before we leave for your practice. Please leave time to do it, and I'll remind you about ten minutes before we need to leave."

### THE KID WHO'S NEVER SATISFIED

**You wanted to treat nine-year-old Ricky to a fun day with a friend. You took the boys to their favorite hamburger place for lunch, let them each play two video games, and then took them to the latest kids' movie (complete with popcorn and a drink for each boy). On the way home, Ricky suggests stopping for ice cream. When you tell him, "Not today, honey," he angrily accuses you of never doing anything nice for him and then pouts the rest of the afternoon.**

When you get home, talk to Ricky about his attitude. Tell him that it hurts your feelings when you do nice things for him and then he notices only what you *don't* do. Let him know that it will be a while before you decide to treat him again. If you feel strongly about it, you might even give him some negative consequence that evening for his poor manners.

Whatever you do, don't take it personally when your child acts as if he can never be satisfied. Remember that children are very egocentric, meaning that they want what they want when they want it. Your job is to see that this attitude is tempered with consideration for other people as your child matures and that you don't reinforce this attitude by giving in to his every request. But don't worry that he has some terrible character defect for trying to get everything his way!

### The Whiner

**Six-year-old Mona is driving you nuts. She whines whenever she wants something and continues even longer if she doesn't get her way. You've just given her the fourth time-out for whining this morning and now you're thinking, "This kid is going to have to spend her whole life in time-out!"**

Since whining has become such a habit for Mona, she probably doesn't even know when she's doing it. It's one of those behaviors you'll have to call to her attention "after the fact."

Bring Mona out of time-out and tell her you want to talk with her about her whining. Ask if she even knows what you mean by the word and ask her to give you some recent examples. If she's unsure, demonstrate by whining to her (not sarcastically, but in the spirit of fun). Then ask her to give you examples of how she *could* say the whiny sentences in an appropriate way without whining. You might label this for her as "talking in her six-year-old voice" rather than talking like a baby.

Once your child clearly understands the definition of whining, tell her that you've come up with a plan to help her stop doing it. Whenever she whines you're going to remind her by saying something like "Could you say that in your six-year-old voice?" If Mona repeats her statement *without* whining, you'll answer her; if not, you won't answer her until she talks appropriately.

Plan to use this system for several days just to make sure Mona understands when she is whining. After this is working well, then tell her you're in phase two of teaching her not to whine. Since she now knows what whining is and has practiced correcting it, you will no longer give her a warning by asking her to repeat her statement in a more grown-up voice. Tell her that when she whines you'll simply ignore her comment until she says it appropriately.

If your child should have a tantrum when you correct her or ignore her, send her to time-out until she's ready to stop throwing a tantrum. You might also want to boost her success rate by offering some incentive for her remembering not to whine. (A poker chip system works well: A parent dispenses a chip when the child uses an appropriate voice, and the child earns a special privilege or inexpensive treat after a specified number of chips.)

### The Negative Child

**Eleven-year-old Janice seems to be in a chronic funk. She complains continually, and nothing ever seems to please her. When the family wants to do something fun, she doesn't think it's fun. When everyone else is having a good time, she looks unhappy. You feel fed up with having her rain on everyone's parade!**

Have a serious talk with Janice about her negative attitude. You might begin by asking her if she knows what "being negative" means. Then give her a simple demonstration: Ask her to play along with you and to follow some simple instruction (like getting the newspaper and placing it on the coffee table). When she does it, smile and thank her for doing it. Then ask her to do the same thing again. This time when she places the paper on the table, be critical ("Why did you put the paper on that side of the table instead of the other? Why didn't you wipe the dust off the table before you put the paper down? Why didn't you fold the paper correctly before placing it on the table?).

Then ask Janice how she felt from your two different reactions. Or you might say something like "The second one felt pretty lousy, didn't it?" Explain that you were giving her an example of "being negative" and that the uncomfortable way she felt during your second demonstration is just how other people in the family feel when *she's* being negative.

If Janice agrees that she's willing to work on being less negative, you might suggest playing a simple game over the next week or two. Establish a signal (such as pulling your right earlobe) that you will give her when she is being negative. Her job is to say something positive immediately. For example, if she comes to the dinner table and says, "Yuck, are we having chicken *again?*" you give her the signal. At that point she'd need to say something like "But I really like the rolls you fixed."

Although this "game" is artificial, it's a great way to help a negative person see how negative she's being. Since everyone usually laughs when she has to make the positive statement, the grumpy one gets great reinforcement for being positive.

In addition to these tactics, notice if you—or someone else in the family—has been unwittingly reinforcing your child's negativity. Does she hear someone being critical of others, perhaps making negative comments about neighbors, colleagues, or the television news? Remember, modeling negativity for a youngster can have a powerful influence on her.

Typically, the family of a negative youngster has gotten into the habit of bending over backward to try to get that child into a good mood. They'll walk on eggshells not to upset her, coddle her with "what's the matter, honey?" when she looks unhappy, and continue to think of compromises to get her to agree with a plan. All of this attention, of course, only reinforces the negative behavior.

Instead, when a child is being negative, ignore her behavior and move on to talk with other people. If she's putting such a damper on a group activity that she's spoiling things for everyone, ask her to go to her room until she's ready to come out and be pleasant and cooperative.

### The Kid Who Has to Have the Last Word

**Ten-year-old Tina is a master at arguing. No matter what you tell her, she always has to have the last word. Now you've just sent her to her room for hitting her brother. She's still shouting, "This isn't fair!" as she slams the door!**

The answer to this dilemma is simple: Let Tina have the last word! Why fight her for it when it doesn't mean anything? What *does* count is the parental control that you've established by sending the child to her room in the first place.

Parents have leverage because of their ability to control many aspects of their children's lives. They can permit—and take away—all sorts of privileges; they can set—and relinquish—all sorts of limits. Words just don't mean that much.

Realize that if your child perpetually argues, someone else must be arguing also. A person simply can't have an argument with herself. The parent who finds herself caught up in arguments with a child has fallen into the trap of believing that an adult must convince a child that the adult is right by having the last word.

Instead, tell your child when you don't want to discuss a topic anymore and then *don't discuss it!* If your youngster persists in hassling you about the subject, tell her to take a time-out until she's ready to drop the subject.

### The Child Who Lies

**You had given ten-year-old Parker permission to go to the mall for the afternoon with his friend Todd and Todd's mother. About an hour before Parker is supposed to return, you get a call from Todd's mother wanting to know what time you're bringing her son home. It seems each boy had told his mother that the other mother would be supervising the mall trip! Murder is illegal, so what do you do instead?**

When Parker returns home, let him know immediately that Todd's mother called and that both of you are wise to the clever little scheme. After Parker tells you where he's been and answered all your questions, set an appropriate negative consequence for his lying as well as for his breaking your rule forbidding him to go to a place without parental supervision (perhaps four to seven days of restriction for each offense).

Typically—but wrongheadedly—a parent might handle this situation by *not* letting the child know she is aware of the lie as soon as she sees him. Instead, she would feign innocence and ask him a series of questions ("How was the mall?" "Did Todd's mom have a good time?"). The child, of course, would probably cover the initial lie with several more until the parent clued him in about the call from Todd's mother.

In this scenario the child typically digs himself into a hole, ending up telling several lies. The parent, of course, becomes even more infuriated as the youngster continues to heap lie upon lie.

Realize that most youngster who have lied (like most adults!) will not admit it until they are absolutely sure that someone has the goods on them. This doesn't mean the youngster is becoming a sociopath or has had a rotten upbringing; it simple means that kids will try to save face (and keep from facing negative consequences) by hanging on to their lie "just in case" the parent might not really know what's going on. To save your child from lowering his self-esteem even more by telling several lies in addition to the original—and to spare a rise in your own blood pressure—it's best to be up-front with your child right from the start.

Ideally, you do want to teach your youngster that it's better for him to admit the truth right away, before you let him know you're wise to his scam, than to lie until he's caught. But many parents get caught in a trap trying to implement this: If a child admits the truth, the parent thinks he must reward the admission by not setting any consequence for the original misdeed; yet the parent might have an uneasy feeling because the misdeed really does require some consequence.

To eliminate this bind, make it clear that there's a negative consequence for a misdeed and *another* consequence for lying about it. For example, a child might get his bike taken away for a week for riding it into another neighborhood against the rules; however if he lied about it as well, his bike would be taken away for two weeks. This is an effective method for putting some meat into the advice that "it's always better to tell the truth."

You'll also want to let your child know the worst consequence of his lying: It has broken your trust in him. Explain the importance of trust in a relationship, and that such a precious commodity is easy to lose, but takes time to rebuild. Tell him specifically what he'll need to do to regain your trust, leaving him with a clear message that you're expecting him to do so.

# CHAPTER 9

## *Threats and Challenges*

Even the calmest, most rational parent can become totally infuriated when her own child threatens her or challenges her parental authority. The instinctive reaction of many parents is "It's just not supposed to be that way!"

Actually, when a child begins to say no (somewhere around eighteen months to age two) parents should celebrate. Why? Because that child is beginning to define his sense of self. Remember that in infancy a baby experiences no boundaries; he literally feels himself to be a part of his mother (or other caretaker) and doesn't distinguish himself as a separate entity apart from her.

Those first no's reveal that the youngster is beginning to see himself as a separate person complete with personal preferences. Just because Mom wants him to eat an orange doesn't mean he has to. He is saying to her, "You are you and I am me."

In learning to become separate a youngster begins to test her independence by challenging the grown-ups. If a parent is too permissive and doesn't provide enough limits, the child can become overly impulsive, irresponsible, and/or demanding when she grows up. If the parent is too coercive or rigid and doesn't allow the youngster to disagree or to have any say in decisions that affect her, she can grow up to be overly adaptive or dependent upon the approval of other people, indecisive, and/or critical (of herself and/or others).

So it's not only normal but it's also healthy for children to disagree out loud with their parents. What they need in return is for their parents to accept disagreement (within reason) but to provide appropriate limits on their children's attempts to manipulate or control.

Threats and challenges are inappropriate forms of disagreement, even though most children will make them occasionally. They represent obvious efforts to manipulate or coerce other people. Some threats are even downright frightening ("I'll run away" or I'll kill myself!"). If a parent gives in to these ultimate power plays, she's allowing herself to be a victim of emotional blackmail. But if she holds her ground she might be plagued with fear that her child could follow through with the threat.

No parent really enjoys being threated or challenged. So let's look at some strategies for dealing with these situations so that dignity is maintained by parent and child alike.

### "You Can't Catch Me!"

**Six-year-old Shelby, all dressed up for Sunday school, has grabbed a leaky red indelible marker despite your telling her not to touch it. After she refuses to bring the marker to you, you move to retrieve it. Shelby begins to run around the room squealing, "You can't catch me!" You have visions of spraining your ankle as you chase her across your newly waxed floors in your high heels!**

Don't chase Shelby. She can't go very far anyway and she's more likely to make a mess with the marker if she's darting away from you. When she sees that you aren't up for a chase, she'll stop running.

When Shelby returns to you (or sits down and allows you to walk over to her), take the marker and give her *two* negative consequences: one for picking up the marker after she'd been told not to and the other for running away from you. Explain clearly what each consequence is for.

Obviously you would not want to give a very young child (a toddler) a consequence for running away from you inside the house. And you would certainly chase her if she was outdoors or in an indoor area where she might get hurt. But if she's not in any danger, it's still best not to chase after her and to let her run out of steam on her own.

If an older child runs out of the house when you are having a disagreement with her, it's best not to run after her. Chasing only lets her know she's gotten the upper hand and reinforces the chance that she'll run farther the next time. Let her come back on her own and then follow through with a consequence.

### "You Can't Make Me!"

**Seven-year-old Jonathan has been acting silly and has just knocked over his snack tray complete with peanut shells and apple juice. When you ask him to get a rag and clean the mess up, he shouts, "You can't make me!"**

Assure Jonathan that he's absolutely right—you can't make him do *anything*. However, let him know that you certainly *can* make his life more miserable if he doesn't follow your request.

If Jonathan refuses to clean up the mess in spite of your reply, you might give him a time-out until he's ready to comply with your request. Or you could clean it up yourself and inform him that he's lost some privilege for the day.

It's pointless to get into a battle with your child about whether or not you can force him to do something. Even if you try, you probably won't succeed. Think of the parent who tries to force a child to eat a bite of food. The parent might succeed in getting the food into the child's mouth, but the youngster typically has the last victory by spitting it out or vomiting the food right back up.

Even if you *could* force your child to do what you want in a given situation, what is the point of proving that you're bigger and stronger? What you really want is for the youngster to make the correct choice and do what you've asked when he's in full control of himself, not because he's coerced.

### "I'm Not Kissing You Ever Again!"

**Four-year-old Joe has been in trouble all evening and has earned an early bedtime as a result. As you tuck him in and bend down to give him his good-night kiss, he turns away and says, "I'm not kissing you ever again!"**

Instead of forcing Joe to kiss you, or trying to convince him to change his mind, let him know that you understand his real message: that he's angry with you. You might say something like "Well, honey, I can understand that you might not feel like kissing me right now. I think you're mad at me for making you go to bed early and people don't feel like kissing when they're mad, right?"

Of course, *you* can still kiss *him,* unless he strenuously objects. This will tell him without words that you don't hold his refusal of affection against him.

Sometimes, when a child refuses to kiss a parent the adult's feelings get hurt. If the parent overdramatizes the rejection, her emotional display only gives the youngster a weapon for the future. Children get angry easily and they make up easily. A wise parent will simply take this show of feelings in stride without making a mountain out of a molehill.

### "So Who Cares, Anyway?"

**Ten-year-old Alex has a new computer and playing computer games has become his favorite pastime. When his report card shows a marked drop in grades, you talk with him about ways he can improve and let him know that if he doesn't, you will limit his computer time. The second report card arrives with grades that are even more dismal and the teacher's comment that Alex isn't turning in his homework. When you follow through and set limits on Alex's computer time, he acts nonchalant and says, "So who cares, anyway?"**

Don't let Alex's words fool you. His ploy to save face is to act *as if* he couldn't care less about that computer, but you know that he does. There's no need to look for another privilege to take away from him just because he doesn't seem upset.

Many parents complain that they can't deprive a child of any privileges because there's nothing that matters to that child. They are concerned that their youngster isn't really experiencing a negative consequence unless he makes a big fuss about it. Although it is important to find consequences, and incentives, that really matter to your youngster, don't expect that he will grant you the pleasure of seeing his distress!

### "You Don't Love Me!"

**When seven-year-old Jessica refuses to pick up her toys in the family room, you tell her that she can't watch any television until the toys are put back in their proper places. Rather than running to put away the toys, she begins to cry and says, "You don't love me!"**

Tell Jessica something like "We're not talking about love right now, Jessica. We're talking about your putting away your toys. Now get in there and get to work on them!" This tactic shows your youngster that you won't fall for her age-old distraction technique.

Another suitable response might be "Come on, Jessica, you know I love you. Now get those toys!" This message makes the issue of love an understood thing but doesn't forget the purpose of the conversation.

Of course, many parents will immediately try to prove that they do, indeed, love the child. They'll cite examples of nice things they've done for her that week, defensively trying to convince her that she's well loved. If the child gets lucky, the parent will get so caught up in the "love talk" that the child won't have to put away her toys!

### "You'll Be Sorry!"

**Nine-year-old Josie has a trashed room and you've given her an ultimatum: Clean it up before two o'clock or you're not going to your best friend's birthday party. In reply Josie coolly turns to you and with dead seriousness says, "You'll be sorry!"**

Let Josie's comment pass for the moment. If you react to it and demand to know why she's threatening you, you'll only encourage her to make such remarks again. She's probably just expressing her anger and really has no intention of retaliating against you.

If Josie remains cool toward you for several hours, however, talk with her about why she's staying so angry. Tell her that you think something's going on between the two of you besides the room hassle and encourage her to tell you about it.

When the two of you are on good terms again, you could mention Josie's earlier threat toward you. Tell her that such remarks make you feel very uncomfortable since they imply that she plans to get even with you. Let her know that each of you will certainly get mad at the other many times in the future, but that the two of you can always talk honestly about what's bothering you and try to work out a mutually agreeable solution. Revenge is never a good way to solve any conflict.

### "I'LL RUN AWAY!"

**Things have been a little tense lately with eleven-year-old Lucy. She seems easily irritated with you and becomes irrationally resentful when you give her advice or tell her she can't do something she wants to do. Now you have to tell her that you will not allow her to wear the eye makeup that she just bought with her allowance. To your horror, she proclaims, "Well, I'm going to run away!" and races upstairs to pack her bag.**

Go to Lucy and tell her that you do not want her to run away now or ever. Let her know that all families have disagreements and that all kids get mad at some of the rules their parents make for them. But there is room for conflict and anger in a family and nobody has to leave because of it.

You might say something like "Lucy, no matter how mad you might get with me or with Dad, we can always work things out. It might take time and we might not agree on everything, but this is your home. You never need to leave your family just because you're angry."

When many parents are faced with this situation, they'll try to call the child's bluff. For example, they'll ask if they can help pack the child's bag for her. Other parents try to use a rational, intellectual approach by pointing out practical problems like "Well, honey, how will you eat? Where will you sleep? Who's going to wash your clothes? You only have enough money to buy four candy bars!" and so on.

The problem with these approaches is that they aren't honest and they can actually make it more likely that your child will run away. The youngster who's threatened to run away has already backed herself into a corner. If you act as if you don't care if she leaves home, or if you try to tease her by making light of her threat, or if you don't respect the seriousness of her statement, she's more likely to run away, if only as a way to save face and try to force you to take her seriously. Even if she doesn't run away, she's likely to have the lingering suspicion that perhaps you really would like it if she weren't around.

No matter how furious you are at your child, you really want her to stay with you. So tell her the truth: that you don't want her to run away, under any circumstances.

### "I'll Kill Myself!"

**Ten-year-old Oscar played hooky from school the other day and you've grounded him for the weekend, including the school carnival he was looking forward to attending. He starts yelling that you're unfair to him and that he can never do anything right. As he runs down the hall to his room he screams, "I'll just kill myself!"**

Go to Oscar immediately and tell him that you're very concerned that he would say he would kill himself. Ask him if he's thought about killing himself, and if so, if he's thought about how he would do it. What you're trying to do, of course, is ascertain just how seriously your child might be considering such a thing.

You might feel certain that your youngster talked of killing himself just to get you upset, and that he wasn't at all serious. And you might be right. The problem is that you don't know for sure until you check it out.

Sometimes your child will reply that he really has thought about killing himself or that he sometimes wishes he were dead. If this is the case, make an appointment immediately with a mental health professional (even if you think you've talked your child out of it and he's promised not to do it).

If your first hunch was correct—that your child was just making this up to get you upset—you'll still want to talk with him about the seriousness of such a threat. Let him know that it isn't at all funny to tell someone you're thinking of killing yourself and that it's a very mean thing to threaten to another person. Remind him that everybody gets angry sometimes, even mad enough to say really scary things. But when everybody cools down and talks things out, things can be worked out.

Remember that in the heat of a situation, a parent is likely to forget all about the fact that the child was grounded. Unless you determine that your child *is* seriously thinking of killing himself, you would still want to reinforce your original consequence. You wouldn't want him to think he could manipulate you by threatening suicide every time he gets in trouble.

By taking your child's statement seriously and checking it out, you give him the message that suicide is very serious business and that you'd never want him to consider it.

# CHAPTER 10

## *Family Problems*

It can happen in any family. There can be some type of sensitive situation or issue that either you or your child will find awkward or even embarrassing.

For example, your child might point out something that is going on within the family (family arguments) that you find difficult to explain. Or she might need your help to cope with a family problem (bankruptcy) that has become public. She might not understand that some family issues are confidential and unwittingly reveal a family secret (your older daughter came home drunk). If you are divorced, you might find yourself dealing with some sensitive issues that are unique to your circumstances (your child doesn't want to visit her other parent).

Let's look at how you might cope with some of these awkward situations that can put you "on the spot" if they should occur in your family.

### "PLEASE DON'T FIGHT!"

**It's late at night and you and your spouse are having a loud argument in the bedroom. Suddenly six-year-old Carol walks in crying and pleads, "Mommy and Daddy, please don't fight!"**

Go over to Carol, put your arms around her, and say something like "It's okay, honey. Daddy and I just get mad at each other sometimes. But we still love each other. There's nothing to worry about." Then take her back to her bed and tuck her in for the remainder of the night.

Some parents might try to cover up the fact that they were fighting, denying that they were angry and basically telling the child that she didn't hear what she heard. This tactic is dishonest and can lead to a trust problem between you and your child. Youngsters intuitively know to believe a person's physiology and body language above his words. Also a much healthier message is to let children know that people who love one another do disagree and argue, sometimes loudly.

Other parents might try to cover up the fact that they're angry by immediately dismissing the child from the bedroom and hustling her back to bed without the benefit of any explanation. It's as if they hope she'll just forget all about the incident by morning. What the child learns by these approaches is that she's not supposed to question her parents when something bothers her and that angry feelings are not to be acknowledged.

Since it isn't appropriate to get into a lengthy discussion with your child in the middle of your argument with your spouse (not to mention the fact that it is the middle of the night!), you should bring the incident up for discussion the next day or soon thereafter. Ask your youngster about her fantasies and feelings when she hears you and your mate arguing, and then give her the necessary reassurance she needs to feel secure. Remind her that all people who love and care for one another will disagree at times, and that it's much better to bring your feelings out into the open rather than to pretend that nothing is wrong. This conversation will not only help your youngster to accept that parental disagreements are normal, but it will also give her the message that it's okay for her to talk about her own angry feelings. Be sure to reassure her that you and your mate have made up and are no longer mad at each other, if that's true. However, if you and your mate are going through a bad time and fighting a lot, don't fake a reconciliation for your child. Simply tell her that the two of you are having a hard time, but that you are working on your problems and will solve them soon.

Of course, if your arguing with your mate is very loud and intense, realize that your child is going to remain frightened no matter what you tell her. Even though there may be no physical violence at all, your child might well worry that there *could be* if either one or both of you are screaming and/or being verbally abusive. Such fighting can be very destructive to a child's sense of security, as would actual physical abuse. Professional counseling might be in order not only for you and your mate, but also for your youngster, in order to help her process her feelings.

### The Innocent Blunderer

**You're having dinner at your in-laws' house when eight-year-old Kay says, "Grandfather, Mommy says you never could keep a job when Daddy was growing up. Why couldn't you?"**

Although your first wish might be to magically disappear, you have several more practical options. One would be to simply let Grandfather answer the question in whatever way he chooses. If he's a fairly open person, he might talk about whatever circumstances prevented him from working steadily. Later, you'd talk to Kay about the inappropriateness of asking someone a question that could embarrass that person, particularly in front of others.

Another choice might be to say something immediately to her such as "Kay, that might be something Grandpa really doesn't want to discuss right now," or "Kay, Grandpa had some bad luck about jobs when your dad was growing up, but it really isn't polite to ask about this right now."

If Grandpa is obviously upset by your child's question, tell him, "I'm sorry, Dad. Kay didn't mean to upset you." To Kay you might then say, "Honey, we'll discuss this later." Change the subject and go on with dinner as usual.

When Grandfather isn't present, you'll want to explain to your child why you reacted the way you did. This discussion would include the fact that a person needs to be careful what she asks about someone's personal history, especially when other people are listening. Many people are very private and don't want to discuss events in their past that might have made them feel inadequate or uncomfortable. Your youngster might better understand this if you can give her an example from her own life: "Kay, you wouldn't want me to ask you in front of other people to talk about something you did or didn't do that you feel badly about (the day you cheated on a test in school, your bed-wetting, the day you took some candy from a store in the mall, and so on), would you?

### The Family Secret Teller

**You're horrified to hear that eight-year-old Patrick has overheard a conversation at home and is now telling his friends at school about his sixteen-year-old sister's coming home drunk the night before.**

Whenever private information has been revealed, don't try to "undo" the damage—you'll probably make it worse! Your best bet is to use the situation to explain to Patrick the importance of confidentiality.

Let Patrick know you are aware that he has spoken about a confidential matter and that, although he probably didn't realize it, he made a big mistake. Explain that people have problems or get themselves caught up in situations that are very private and personal and that it's important for those who care about them to keep such information confidential. His telling about his sister's coming home drunk was revealing something that only she should have the right to reveal.

Explain that if someone in the family is having a personal problem, another family member should not casually talk about it without permission from the one who has the problem. Family members need to be loyal to one another, to support one another, and to have respect for one another's feelings.

You'll also have to help Patrick with what he should say in the future if someone brings up the subject of his sister's drinking. One appropriate response might be "I really don't want to talk about it because it's a personal matter."

### "How Can You Do That to Me?"

**Ten-year-old Andy comes home from school and tells you he learned about research showing that secondhand smoke is dangerous to everyone who has to breathe it. He asks, "If you know you can give me cancer, Mom, why won't you stop smoking?"**

You don't have much choice but to acknowledge that your child's information is correct. And, darn it, he has a good point! So now what do you do?

Of course, one logical option would be to quit smoking. If it's out of the question for you to consider quitting, explain this to your child. For example, you might tell him that you've tried to quit smoking in the past but have never been successful. Or (if it's true) that you plan to quit at some point in the future but the timing isn't right for this yet. If you feel powerlessly addicted, this would be a good time to let your youngster know about this as a potential lesson to keep him from ever starting to smoke.

In addition to sharing your feelings about the subject, if you aren't willing to quit smoking, why not work out a compromise. Tell your child that the information about secondhand smoke is frightening and that you certainly don't want to jeopardize his health. Let him know that you will smoke outside (or perhaps in a designated "smoking room") out of consideration for the health of the rest of your family.

### "What Do You Mean There's No Money?"

**Your financial circumstances are such that you can't send eleven-year-old Emily to the summer camp she's been attending the past few years. What do you tell her and how do you help her handle this problem with her friends?**

Remember that one of the jobs of being a good parent is to prepare your child to cope with unpleasant or upsetting circumstances. Your honesty with her at this time will set a positive example for her even if the situation is uncomfortable.

Explain your financial situation to Emily, telling her the essence of the problem without going into too much detail. For instance, remind her of some change in circumstances that led to the difficulty, such as a cut in income, greater expenses, and so on. Then tell her that everyone in the family has to make sacrifices to cut expenses and give her examples of some things you are doing to save money. Bring up the camp issue and let her know that you feel badly that she will have to give up going to camp this year.

If she becomes angry, acknowledge that you can understand her feelings. It's perfectly normal to get mad when things don't happen the way one would like them to. However, feelings don't change the situation. Let your child know that you expect her to understand your plight and to cooperate with you in spite of her anger.

As for what she should tell her friends, let her know that there's really nothing wrong in stating that the money for camp just isn't there this year. Let her frame the situation in a positive way by helping her be truthful without embarrassing her or anyone else in the family. For example, rather than saying, "Mom got fired," she could say, "My mom isn't working right now," or she could say something more general like "Our family has just had too many other expenses this year."

If information about your family's financial circumstances has become public (your child's classmates somehow know you've filed for bankruptcy, for example), give your child something positive to say in the event that she's confronted by her peers about the situation. This can be a simple statement such as "Yes, my family had some bad luck this past year," or "Yes, my parents have had a lot of extra expenses lately, so we're cutting down on our spending right now."

To help your child feel more positive when you're having financial problems, let her know that you'll begin exploring ways the family can have fun together without it costing a lot of money. Picnics, hiking, and trips to museums and craft shows are a few examples. And don't forget about board and card games for those evenings at home.

## "Dad, Mommy Was Drunk!"

**When you arrive home from work, you find eight-year-old Howard crying in his room. When you ask him what's wrong, he tells you that the cookies burned in the oven because Mommy fell asleep from drinking too much wine.**

Tell Howard that you're very sorry this happened and that you'll discuss the situation with Mommy. Talk to Howard to see if he has been aware of any similar incidents (assuming you haven't had this discussion before). Be sensitive to the fact that he might be worried that he's tattled on his mother when he shouldn't. Reassure him that it's okay to tell either parent anything that's bothering him, and that you'll handle the situation with his mother.

The point is that you don't want to try to deny what your child witnessed. Telling him, "Oh, honey, I'm sure you're exaggerating how much wine Mommy had!" or "Now, Howard, your mother wouldn't do such a thing. You must have just *thought* that she was drinking wine," will only teach your youngster not to talk to you about his concerns in the future.

If your spouse has a drinking problem, you'll want to get professional help before it worsens. If she won't participate, consult with your priest, minister, or rabbi, a local group that deals with alcoholism (Alcoholics Anonymous, Rational Recovery), or a mental health professional about what you can do to help the situation.

### "But It's Okay with Dad!"

**You and your spouse are in your bedroom watching television when eleven-year-old Mary pops in to show you the new swimsuit she bought at the mall with her allowance. To your amazement, your mate compliments Mary on her selection while you're thinking "There's no way I'm going to allow my well-developed daughter to wear that skimpy little bikini!"**

Since Mary already knows how your mate feels about the suit, you're in a bind. Go ahead and speak up about your reservations immediately. You might say something like "Mary, I'm afraid I don't share the same opinion about this. I'm not sure I approve of your wearing a bikini at your age. Your dad and I are going to have to talk this over."

Go ahead and hear whatever Mary has to say on the subject (and she'll probably have plenty) and then tell her you'll consider her opinion. When you and your spouse are alone and have had a little time to think about the matter, see whether or not you both still disagree. If you do disagree, you might consider a compromise: Mary can wear the suit in the privacy of her own home or backyard but not out in public.

If there isn't a compromise that is acceptable to both of you, then one of you obviously must acquiesce to the other. Tell Mary what the two of you have mutually decided: "Your Dad has agreed to abide by my wishes on this, Mary. You'll not be allowed to wear the suit."

This resolution makes it clear that you and your mate can and do differ in your opinions, but that you try as best you can to work things out for a mutually satisfactory decision. If you can't agree or compromise, you're each flexible enough to occasionally give in to the wishes of the other. It also makes it clear that one parent cannot be played off against the other.

## "Can't You Please Get Along?"

**You and your ex aren't speaking after a bitter, nasty divorce. Nine-year-old Ian comes home from school with an invitation for Parents' Night and begs for you and the other parent to attend the function—*together!***

This might be just the occasion to make the decision that you will behave in an adult manner—and will encourage your ex to do likewise—when your child's emotional well-being is involved. Although it might be very difficult for ex-spouses to put their own angry feelings aside, most will agree (in their rational moments) that their youngster should be able to have access to each of them and to see them behave maturely in his presence. After all, a child shouldn't have to deal with tension or embarrassment created by the people who supposedly love him most in the world.

If you decide for whatever reason that you simply will not sit through a social event at your ex's side, consider a compromise. You might tell your child that you want him to invite the other parent and that you will attend, but that you will not choose to sit with your ex. If you and your ex are in this situation, your child is probably already very aware of the animosity between the two of you. So tell him frankly that you and your ex do not want to communicate any more than is absolutely necessary and that he'll have to accept that fact. But you will still go to Parents' Night, and you will encourage your child to invite your ex as well.

If you and your ex do not even want to be in the same room together, tell your child that you think it's best that *both* of you not go to the same function. Suggest that you and your ex will take turns attending special functions, and be gracious enough to accept the rotation without complaining or making guilt-inducing remarks to your youngster when it's your turn to forfeit a visit. It's to be hoped that both you and your ex eventually will be able to get along well enough so you don't have to rotate your offspring's graduation(s) or wedding!

### "I Want a New Daddy!"

**It's your first date after your divorce. When your date arrives, five-year-old Blair rushes to the door, bear-hugs him, and asks, "Will you please be my new daddy so my mommy won't be so lonely?"**

Rattled as you might feel, try to make your date a little more comfortable by jokingly saying something like "Well, I don't think we're quite ready for that!" Then change the subject and proceed to get your date and your child acquainted in the way you'd already intended. Save further comment about Blair's remark until you and she are alone. Your date will probably appreciate and admire your light attitude about this and will be glad you didn't make him a witness (or participant) in some heavy discussion with your child about male-female relationships.

Before you talk to your youngster about this incident, give some thought to what her comment might signify about her current emotional state. Realize that it's unlikely she acted out of a wish to embarrass you, but was probably naïvely expressing her underlying neediness.

Is she having enough contact with her father? If this cannot be increased for some reason, is there a grandfather, uncle, or male friend who might be willing to establish regular, frequent contact with her? If none of these options is available, perhaps you can enroll her in activities where she will have a male role model (a teacher at your church/synagogue or school, a gymnastics or athletic coach, and so on).

Also ask yourself if you've been giving your child, intentionally or not, the impression that you are terribly unhappy and/or needy. Is her plea for a new daddy her way to try to take care of you?

If you are having a tough time dealing with loneliness, take an objective look at your own support network. If you don't have one, actively plan to change this situation by seeking out activities or groups that you might enjoy. You also might consider joining a support group for singles or talking things over with a psychotherapist.

When you talk to Blair about her behavior with your date, let her know that her remark was inappropriate by telling her how you *want* her to act when you introduce her to a man. This includes telling her what to say as well as what not to say. Explain (if it's true) that you might like to get married some day but that a man and woman must get to know each other very well before they make such an important decision. Draw her out about how you think she's feeling about her father or about not having him around.

If you get the feeling your child is more concerned about your emotional needs, acknowledge that you've been feeling sad or upset but that you are finding ways to change the situation. Give her the reassurance that even if you aren't married you still are able to take care of her. While it might be nice to have a "daddy" in the house, it's not a necessity.

### "I Don't Want to Go See Daddy!"

**It's time for seven-year-old Teddy to board the airplane to spend the Christmas holidays with your ex. Suddenly he begins to cry, says he wants to stay with you, and begs you not to make him go.**

Comfort Teddy as best you can, but the bottom line is to get him on that plane. Just as with any other type of separation problem, remember that a child is very likely to calm down once you are out of sight. You might also want to board the plane with your child and get him settled in his seat, if it's allowed. Although it's very difficult (especially since you probably wish he didn't have to go either), remind him about when you will see him again.

Then tell him you want him to have a good time, kiss him goodbye, and leave the plane. The airline staff will take over at that point.

Remember that it's best for your child to carry out planned visits with the other parent whenever possible. Not only will you avoid making your ex think you're negatively influencing your child, but you'll also be letting your youngster know that you do support the visit. Even if you're really not wanting him to go but are being made by the court to carry this out, you'll create less stress for your child by actively supporting the court's decision (at least in front of him).

Of course there are some things you can do *before* the day of departure that can lessen the likelihood that this problem will occur. You'll want to remind your child, if he doesn't remember, about good times he's had when he's visited your ex before. Point out (if it's true) that he usually gets upset right before he leaves you but then goes on to have a really good time. Talk with him about how he might prevent himself from getting so upset. For example, he might feel more secure about leaving if he has a little calendar marking the day he'll return to see you. Or he might want to take your picture or some special item of yours with him to comfort himself. Write down your phone numbers; even though you know your ex has them, your child might feel more secure having his own.

The other part of preparing your child for visiting the other parent is to look at the messages you send out about his leaving you. You want him to know that you'll miss having him around, but you don't want to burden him with worrying that you'll be miserable without him. If you send the message, even subtly, that you're going to be lonely and upset without him, you're setting him up to feel guilty about leaving you. Instead, tell him about some things you're going to be doing or accomplishing while he's gone. You'll be letting him know that he doesn't have to worry about your emotional needs and giving him the unspoken permission he requires to enjoy himself on his visit.

If you and your ex were involved in a custody battle, your child is likely to be aware of that fact. Even if the court's decisions about custody and visitation arrangements are not to your liking, it's best to enact them with as much goodwill as you can muster. Your child might still question why things have to be the way they are. If he does, it's usually best to insist matter-of-factly that the court's wishes must be followed. If you behave as if the child might have some choice over the matter, you can leave him with anxiety about a power he doesn't really have.

## CHAPTER 11

# *Just a Minute! That's* My *Child!*

Just about every parent will have the frustrating experience of having her child falsely accused of some wrongdoing. When it's playground stuff, kids teasing kids, it's probably better to let the youngster work things out on his own without any parental interference—unless he's in physical danger. But when the unfairness is generated by an adult, a parent might need to go to bat for her child's best interests.

Obviously the other adult may well perceive you as an overprotective, naïve, and/or totally biased parent. But the question remains: Who else will take up for your child? Sometimes you just have to take a stand in spite of how it might appear to other people.

Now take a look at some of the situations in which another adult might put you on the spot about your child.

### The Misinformed Teacher

**Eight-year-old David was diagnosed with a learning difference when he was in first grade. He has trouble tracking visually and needs to have written instructions given to him at his desk rather than having to copy them from the board. Unfortunately, his teacher insists that he must copy from the board and tells him that he just needs to "try harder."**

Call for an appointment with the teacher and take any of David's relevant test results or other diagnostic records with you to the conference. Tell the teacher that you'd like her to look over this material because it relates to David's difficulty in copying from the board.

Although the material you bring to the conference might be a part of your child's school records, realize that many teachers simply don't have the time to go through all of this material. The teacher may not have not known about your son's problem and may be quite willing to help once she has the correct information.

If the teacher tells you that she can't change the rules of her classroom for one child, ask her if she'd be willing to try it for a couple of weeks. Let her know how other teachers have successfully coped with this problem. Tell her that if she could see the improvement in David's performance from this one change in her routine, you feel sure she would continue to give him his written instructions at his seat.

Remain positive and make the assumption that the teacher has her heart in the right place. But if your efforts with her get nowhere, ask for a conference with the school principal and/or counselor.

### The Problem Teacher

**Seven-year-old Dillon is a timid, insecure child who has developed sleep problems and morning stomachaches before school. The pediatrician has checked him out and told you that Dillon's condition is stress-related. When Dillon finally tells you what's bothering him, he says that his teacher scares him because she yells at youngsters when they don't give her the right answer or when they don't seem to be paying attention. After some checking with other parents who have children in the same class, you find out Dillon is telling the truth about his teacher's lack of verbal control.**

Schedule a conference with the teacher and talk with her candidly about the problem. Let her know up-front that several other children are reporting the same thing about her yelling in class. It's just possible that she'll do some self-examination and make some changes as a result of your bringing this to her attention.

If the problem continues, talk with the school counselor and/or principal. At this point it might help to have some other parents go with you. Unless the problem is corrected, insist that your child be placed in another teacher's classroom.

Realize that a parent should not insist on a classroom change on a whim or without first trying to work out a solution with the current teacher. But it's a parent's right to remove her child from a classroom of a teacher who yells, puts children down with careless remarks, or is harsh in her classroom management.

### The Unwelcome Disciplinarian

**You've taken four-year-old Janie to play with your friend's preschooler. As you and your friend are chatting, Janie picks up a fragile knickknack from the coffee table. Your friend jumps up, grabs Janie by the arm, swats her behind, and tells her to leave the things on the coffee table alone.**

Tell your friend that you're sorry Janie picked up the item but that you prefer to discipline her yourself when the four of you are together. Acknowledge that everyone has a different idea about how to raise kids but that you've decided not to use spankings with Janie. Tell her that you would prefer it if she'd follow your wishes on this matter should you not be around when Janie does something that requires discipline. Then let her know what action you would take, such as giving Janie a time-out in a nearby chair.

If Janie is persistent about touching items, tell your friend that you'd like to put the objects on the coffee table out of your child's reach and then replace them before you leave. Let your friend know that this will give both of you peace of mind during the visit.

### The Upset Neighbor

**Nine-year-old Bart and some of the other boys on the block often throw a football in the cul-de-sac. One afternoon you hear a cranky neighbor loudly bawling Bart out for throwing the ball into her rose bed. You understand your neighbor's frustration over the incident but sympathize with your son's embarrassment and anger over being severely bawled out in front of his friends.**

Tell Bart that you think the neighbor acted inappropriately in chastising him in front of his peers but that he must take responsibility for throwing the ball into the rose bed. Ask him to apologize to the neighbor for the ball's accidentally squashing her flowers. If you have a backyard or if there's a playground or open field nearby, encourage him to play ball in one of those areas. If there isn't a place like that, warn him about being careful in the future to avoid kicking the ball in a direction where it could do damage to someone's yard or house.

If there continues to be tension between the neighbor and your child, you'll need to check on the legal issues that are involved.

Should you find that your child is within his legal rights for whatever the neighbor is complaining about, you'll need to clarify that with her rather than expecting him to do it.

Of course, even if your child technically has the right to do whatever he's doing, you might want to ask him to concede to the neighbor's wishes in order to promote peace within the neighborhood. Youngsters need to learn the value of being flexible and conceding on some issues for the good of a system (unless doing so violates a very basic ethical or moral principle).

### "I Didn't Do It!"

**The ballet teacher calls to tell you that ten-year-old Colette has been accused of stealing another child's gold locket. When you tell Colette about the call, she adamantly insists that it was another child who stole the locket, that she has explained this to the teacher, but that the teacher doesn't believe her.**

If Colette is not a child who lies to you and if she has no history of stealing, you might feel pretty sure that she's telling you the truth. Of course the problem is more complicated if Colette ever *has* stolen or lied, although she could still be innocent in this case.

If Colette's story still seems believable after you've listened to her explanation, go ahead and let the ballet teacher know that you don't believe that your child stole the locket. Obviously you run the risk of being wrong (and you'd certainly tell the teacher you were wrong if you find this out), but you run an even greater risk of losing your child's trust in you if you act as if you believe she's lying.

In general, get all the information you can get, evaluate it objectively, and then support your child if you have nothing to convince you that she's not telling you the truth. If you find out you were wrong and that your child lied, you would not support her the next time and you would use the opportunity to teach her that it's difficult to trust once trust has been broken.

### "But I Don't Believe That!"

**Nine-year-old Jackie has been best friends with Beth since the two girls were very young. Now Beth's parents have gotten into a new religion with beliefs that are very different from yours, and they are trying to convince your child to reject your beliefs.**

While this could be a ticklish situation, you have little choice but to confront Beth's parents with your concerns. It's probably better to do this in person rather than to attempt it over the telephone.

Tell Beth's parents that you value the friendship the girls have had over the years (and your friendship with them as well, if you have one) but you have a concern that is bothering you. Let them know that you want your child to respect other people's religious convictions but that you want your beliefs to be respected as well. Tell them in a nonaccusing manner that you understand they've been talking to your child lately about their beliefs, and that their views conflict directly with some of yours. For the sake of everyone concerned, you'd like the two families to agree not to try to convert either child's beliefs to those of the other family.

Realize that no matter how tactfully and sensitively you present your thoughts about this situation, there is a risk that the other family will not allow the girls' friendship to continue, at least not at the same level of intensity. If this happens, you'll need to let your child know that the other family apparently decided to end or change the friendship after you asked them not to try to convert her to their religion.

If she loses contact with her friend, she'll probably be sad about it and you'll want to empathize with her loss. She might even be angry with you for confronting her friend's family, in which case you can tell her you're sorry she's angry with you, but you felt you had to do what you did. Let her know that you are sorry the other family reacted the way they did to your request, and that it was not your intention to change her friendship with the other child. This would be a good time to let her know that sometimes a person can lose a friend by standing up for a principle.

# *Suggested Readings*

## FOR PARENTS

Babcock, Dorothy E., and Terry D. Keepers. *Raising Kids OK.* New York: Avon, 1977.

Craig, Judi. *Little Kids, Big Questions.* New York: Hearst Books, 1993.

Dodson, Fitzhugh. *How to Parent.* New York: New American Library, 1971.

———. *How to Father.* New York: New American Library, 1978.

Dreikurs, Rudolf. *Coping with Children's Misbehavior.* New York: Hawthorn Books, Inc., 1972.

———, and Loren Gray. *A Parent's Guide to Child Discipline.* New York: Hawthorn Books, Inc., 1970.

Eckler, James D. *Step-by-Step Parenting.* White Hall, Va: Betterway Publications, 1988.

Elkind, David. *The Hurried Child.* Reading, Mass.: Addison-Wesley Publishing Co., Inc., 1988.

Faber, Adele, and Elaine Maglish. *How to Talk So Kids Will Listen and Listen So Kids Will Talk.* New York: Avon, 1982.

Garber, Stephen W., Marianne Garber, and Robyn Spizman. *Good Behavior.* New York: Villard Books, 1987.

Gardiner, Richard A. *The Parents Book About Divorce.* New York: Creative Therapeutics, 1977.

———. *Understanding Children: A Parent's Guide to Child-Rearing.* New York: Creative Therapeutics, 1979.

Ginot, Haim G. *Between Parent and Child.* New York: Avon, 1971.

Gordon, Thomas. *Parent Effectiveness Training.* New York: Peter H. Wyden, Inc., 1973.

Grollman, Earl A. *Explaining Death to Children.* Boston: Beacon Press, 1969.

Ingersol, Barbara. *Your Hyperactive Child.* Garden City, N.Y.: Doubleday & Co., 1988.

Patterson, Gerald R. *Living with Children.* Champaign, Ill.: Research Press, 1968.

———, and Leslie Becker. *Parents Are Teachers.* Champaign, Ill.: Research Press, 1971.

Popkin, Michael. *Active Parenting.* San Francisco, Calif.: Harper & Row, 1987.

Schaefer, Charles E., and Howard L. Millmann. *How to Help Children with Common Problems.* New York: Van Nostrand Reinhold Company, 1981.

Tureki, Stanley K., and Leslie Tonner. *The Difficult Child.* New York: Bantam Books, 1989.

## FOR CHILDREN

Aliki. *Feelings.* New York: Mulberry Books, 1985.

Banish, Roslyn. *A Forever Family.* New York: HarperCollins, 1992.

Brown, Laurene L., and Marc Brown. *Dinosaurs Divorce.* Boston: Little, Brown & Company, 1986.

Brown, Marc, and Stephen Krensky. *Dinosaurs Beware!* Boston: Little, Brown & Company, 1982.

Brown, Tricia. *Someone Special, Just Like You.* New York: Henry Holt & Company, 1982.

Bryan, Mellonie, and Robert Ingpen. *Lifetimes.* New York: Bantam Books, 1983.

Ciliotta, Claire, and Carole Livingston. *Why Am I Going to the Hospital?* Secaucus, N.J.: Lyle Stuart, Inc., 1981.

Clifton, Lucille. *Everett Anderson's Goodbye.* New York: Henry Holt & Company, 1983.

Cole, Joanna. *The New Baby at Your House.* New York: Mulberry Books, 1985.

Cosgrove, Stephen. The *Serendipity Books Series.* Los Angeles: Price Stern Sloan, 1985–1990.

Delton, Judy. *My Mother Lost Her Job Today.* Niles, Ill.: Albert Whitman & Company. 1980.

———. *I'll Never Love Anything Ever Again.* Niles, Ill.: Albert Whitman & Company, 1985.

Dwyer, Kathleen M. *What Do You Mean I Have a Learning Disability?* New York: Walker & Company, 1991.

Fassler, David, and Kelly McQueen. *What's a Virus, Anyway?* Burlington, Vt.: Waterfront Books, 1990.

Freed, Alvyn M. *T.A. for Tots.* Rolling Hills Estates, Calif.: Jalmar Press, 1991

Gardiner, Richard A. *The Boys and Girls Book About Divorce.* New York: Creative Therapeutics, 1977.

———. *Modern Fairy Tales.* Philadelphia: George F. Stickley Company, 1977.

———. *The Boys and Girls Book About Step-Families.* New York: Creative Therapeutics, 1983.

Girard, Linda W. *My Body Is Private.* Niles, Ill.: Albert Whitman & Company, 1984.

———. *Adoption Is for Always.* Niles, Ill.: Albert Whitman & Company, 1986.

Goldman, Rita. *Body Battles.* New York: Scholastic Inc., 1992.

Grollman, Earl A. *Talking About Death: A Dialogue Between Parent and Child.* Boston: Beacon Press, 1991.

Hausherr, Rosmarie. *Children and the AIDS Virus.* New York: Clarion Books, 1989.

Livingston, Carole. *Why Was I Adopted?* New York: Carol Publishing Group, 1990.

Madaras, Lynda. *The What's Happening to My Body? Book for Boys.* New York: Newmarket Press, 1984.

———. *The What's Happening to My Body? Book for Girls.* New York: Newmarket Press, 1988.

Mayle, Peter. *Where Did I Come From?* New York: Carol Publishing Group, 1973.

———. *What's Happening to Me?* New York: Carol Publishing Group, 1990.

———. *What Am I Doing in a Stepfamily?* New York: Carol Publishing Group, 1992.

Moss, Deborah M. *Shelley, The Hyperactive Turtle.* Rockville, Md.: Woodbine House, 1989.

Mursch, Robert, and Sheila McGaaw. *Love You Forever.* Ontario: Firefly Books, 1986.

Palmer, Pat. *The Mouse, the Monster, and Me.* San Luis Obispo, Calif.: Impact Publishers, 1977.

Rogers, Fred. *Making Friends.* New York: G. P. Putnam's Sons, 1987.

———. *Going to the Hospital.* New York: G. P. Putnam's Sons, 1988.

———. *Going to the Dentist.* New York: G. P. Putnam's Sons, 1989.

Sharmat, Marjorie W. *Mitchell Is Moving.* New York: Aladdin Books, 1978.

Simon, Norma. *Why Am I Different?* Niles, Ill.: Albert Whitman & Company, 1976.

———. *The Saddest Time.* Niles, Ill.: Albert Whitman & Company, 1986.

Stein, Sara B. *Making Babies.* New York: Walker & Company, 1974.

Varley, Susan. *Badger's Parting Gifts.* New York: Mulberry Books, 1984.

Vigna, Judith. *I Wish Daddy Didn't Drink So Much.* Niles, Ill.: Albert Whitman & Company, 1988.

Viorst, Judith. *The Tenth Good Thing About Barney.* New York: Macmillan Publishing Company, 1971.

# INDEX


abuse, 134
  by child-care person, 67–68
  physical, 39, 52, 193
  self-, 111–112
  sexual, 52, 126, 147–148
  spanking and, 28
  verbal, 39, 193
accountability, personal, 74–75
accusations, false, 205, 209
active listening, 26
adoption:
  fears and, 165–166
  inappropriate remarks about, 84–85
affection, physical, 23–24, 46
  between parents, jealousy of, 158–159
  rejection of, 79–80, 184
aggressive behavior, 28, 38, 99–114, 148
  toward animals, 105–106
  behavior-modification systems for, 131–133
  biting, 101–103
  hitting a parent, 103–104
  passive-, 112–114
  property damage, 106–107, 171
  saying "I hate you!," 100–101
  in school, 130–133
  self-abuse, 111–112
  among siblings, 35, 108–110
  substitute behaviors for, 102
  tantrums, 30, 34, 63, 104–105, 175
  verbal, 95–96, 100–101, 110–111, 131
alarm clocks, 45–46, 53
alarm devices, for bed-wetting, 53
alcohol abuse, 191, 194–195, 197–198
animals, aggressive behavior toward, 105–106
anticoercive stance, 183–184
anxieties, *see* fears
arguing, 24, 43, 113, 177
  between parents, 191–193
attendance, school, 120–122
attentional problems, 124–126
attention-seeking behavior, 21, 28, 29, 55, 60, 61, 93–94, 105, 109, 124, 138, 170, 176

"bad thoughts," 163–164
ballet dancing, 164–165
baths, 19, 34, 56–57
bedtime, 57, 66, 171
  delaying tactics at, 60–62
  eating problems and, 49
bed-wetting, 51–54
  cause of, 52
  logical consequences of, 53–54
  management of, 52–53
behavior-modification systems, 131–133
biting, 101–103
bladder-training exercises, 53
blaming, 22, 74–75, 162
boredom, 21, 66
bossiness, 96–97
bribery, 33
bullying, 95–96, 130

"card" behavior-modification system, 131
cars, hazardous behavior in, 75–76
chain locks, 170–171

challenges, 50, 113, 181–189
  accusations of unloving attitude, 185–186
  anticoercive stance, 183–184
  asserted indifference, 185
  rejecting physical affection, 184
  running away, 182–183
  *see also* oppositional behavior; threats
changes, adjustment to, 63–64, 65
chart system, 33, 35–36
chattering, 92–93
cheating, 83–84
  peer pressure in, 129–130
  in school, 128–130
child-care person, 67–68, 137
childproof home, 47–48
choices, offering of, 49, 50, 56, 124
chores, 35, 39, 66, 112–113
  cleaning up, 59–60, 171, 183, 185–187
  during school suspension, 136–137
clothing, 198–199
  designer, 78–79, 161–162
communication, 24–26, 136
  listening, 26, 40, 92–93, 94
  positive vs. negative statements in, 25
  teacher-parent, 101–102, 127, 131–133, 135–136
  yelling, 25–26, 37, 61, 124, 207
  *see also* talking
compromise, 81, 87, 195, 198, 199
computer games, 185
confidentiality, 191, 194–195
consequences, *see* logical consequences; negative consequences
cursing, 141–142
custody battles, 202–203

daily routine, 43–68
  adjustment to changes in, 63–64, 65
  baths in, 19, 34, 56–57
  bed-wetting and, 51–54
  boredom and, 66
  child-care person in, 67–68, 137
  "compassionate break" from, 56
  dawdling in, 27, 58–59, 62–63, 123
  getting dressed in, 58–59
  getting up in the morning in, 45–47, 58–59
  offering choices in, 49, 50, 56, 124
  sibling rivalry and, 65–66
  toilet training in, 50–51, 54–56
  touching of household objects and, 47–48
  *see also* bedtime; chores; meals
dating after divorce, 200–201
dawdling, 27, 58–59, 62–63, 123
depression, 126, 133
designer clothing, 78–79, 161–162
dinnertime, 62–63
discipline, 19–41, 136–137
  chart system in, 33, 35–36
  definition of, 21
  egocentrism vs., 21–22, 56, 173–174, 181
  excessive, 22, 32–33, 44, 56, 113–114, 172, 181–182
  face-saving behaviors and, 37–38, 79, 90, 178, 185, 188
  nagging and, 38–39, 57, 60, 128
  parental loss of emotional control in, 39–40
  perspective needed in, 20–21, 22, 39–41
  praise in, 22–24, 26, 40
  purpose of, 22
  security produced by, 22, 28, 44, 172
  spanking as, 27–28
  time limits in, 30, 31–32, 39, 57, 60, 127–128, 170
  *see also* incentives; logical consequences; negative consequences
displacement of anger, 106
divorce, 29, 191, 199–203
  attending events with ex-spouse after, 199–200
  custody battles in, 202–203
  dating after, 200–201
  separation anxiety over visitation after, 201–203
doctors, 153
  bed-wetting and, 52–53
  fear of, 163
  playing, 147–148
  soiling problems and, 55
dressing, 58–59
  *see also* clothing
dressing up, 144–145
driving, hazardous behavior while, 75–76
drug abuse, 126

eating problems, 48–50, 183
educational evaluation, 124–126
egocentrism, 21–22, 56, 173–174, 181
embarrassing remarks, *see* inappropriate remarks
emotional blackmail, 182
enriching educational experiences, 134

face-saving behaviors, 37–38, 79, 90, 178, 185, 188
fairness, 160–161
  unfairness vs., *see* protective reactions, parental
false accusations, 205, 209
family issues, 191–203
  alcohol abuse, 191, 194–195, 197–198

family secrets, 191, 194–195
financial problems, 191, 196–197
inappropriate remarks, 193–194
parental arguments, 191–193
playing off one parent against the other, 198–199
smoking, 195
*see also* divorce
fantasies, 158, 159, 162, 170
about adoption, 165, 166
of imaginary playmate, 72
sexual, 143
fears, 89–90, 151–168, 195, 207
about adoption, 165–166
about "bad thoughts," 163–164
in denying illness, 162–163
of doctors, 163
fairness and, 160–161
of imaginary monsters, 152, 154, 170
inadequate talent and, 164–165
jealousy and, 158–162
nightmares and, 152, 153–155
parental arguments and, 191–193
perfectionism and, 155–156
self-esteem and, 167–168
sleeping in parents' bed because of, 156–157
about team sports, 166–167
feelings, sensitivity to, 73–74, 79–80, 84–86, 110–111
fighting, *see* aggressive behavior
financial problems, 191, 196–197
foul language, 141–142

gender identification, 144–145
genitalia:
masturbation of, 140, 163–164
parent's, viewing of, 143–144
privacy of, 143–144, 147
touching of, 140, 147, 148, 163–164
gifts, acceptance of, 73–74
"goody bag," 37
grounding, 31–32, 188, 189
grumpiness, morning, 45–47

hatred, verbal expression of, 100–101
hitting a parent, 103–104
homework, 19–20, 25, 39, 167
independently completed, 122–124
tutors for, 124, 126
uncompleted, 126–128, 185
household objects, touching of, 47–48, 207–208
hygiene, personal, 19, 34, 56–57
hyperactivity, 125

"I hate you!," 100–101
illness, 70, 195
denial of, 162–163
stress-induced symptoms of, 119–120, 207
imaginary monsters, fear of, 152, 154, 170
imaginary playmates, 72
inappropriate remarks, 19, 21, 81, 84–86
about adoption, 84–85
in family issues, 193–194
about gifts, 73–74
personally offensive, 85–86
about physical affection, 79–80
rudeness and, 73–74, 79–80, 84–86
inappropriate touching, 148
incentives, 33–37, 57, 61, 97, 102, 123, 132, 169
bribery vs., 33
"goody bag," 37
guidelines for, 34–36
objections to, 33–34
poker chips, 36, 175
privileges, 36–37, 131–133, 134
for toilet training, 55
indifference, asserted, 185
interrupting, 35, 158–159

jealousy, 158–162
of parental relationship, 158–159
of siblings, 159–162

kindergarten, 117–118

language, foul, 141–142
lap, parental, 97–98
late bloomers, 134–135
lateness, 34
dawdling and, 27, 58–59, 62–63, 123
learning problems, 124–126, 206
limits, setting of, 21–22, 29, 170, 172, 177, 181, 182, 185
testing of, 21, 43–44, 49, 61
*see also* discipline
listening, 26, 40, 92–93, 94
locks, chain, 170–171
logical consequences, 30–31, 53–55
of bed-wetting, 53–54
of dawdling, 58
of lateness for meals, 62–63
of purposeful soiling, 54–55
loyalty, 195
lying, 67, 68, 75, 128, 135, 177–179, 209

magazines, sexually-oriented, 145–147
masturbation, 163–164
public, 140
meals:
dinnertime, 62–63
eating problems and, 48–50, 183

meals (*cont.*)
  restaurant, 82–83
monsters, imaginary, 152, 154, 170
morning routine, 27, 45–47, 58–59
motivation problems in school, 126–127, 134–135

nagging, 38–39, 57, 60, 128
negative attitude, 175–176
negative consequences, 21, 26, 27–33, 56–57, 76, 77–78, 82, 86, 102, 130, 131–132, 142, 173, 178–179
  denying privileges, 31–33, 128–129, 134, 137, 183, 185
  punishment vs., 27
  spanking, 27–28
  *see also* logical consequences; time-outs
negative touching, 27
negative vs. positive statements, 25
negotiations, 45, 78–79, 81, 87
neighbors, problems with, 110, 208–209
never-satisfied attitude, 173–174
nightmares, 152, 153–155
night terrors, 153
nudity:
  public, 142–143
  sex play and, 147–148

oppositional behavior, 47, 169–179
  arguing, 24, 43, 113, 177
  lying, 67, 68, 75, 128, 135, 177–179, 209
  negative attitude, 175–176
  never-satisfied attitude, 173–174
  time-outs and, 169–172
  tuning out parental requests, 172–173
  whining, 30, 35, 174–175

parties, 89–90
passive-aggressive behavior, 112–114
peer pressure, 79
  in cheating, 129–130
peer relationships, 69–70, 71, 94–97, 168
  aggressive behavior in, 130–133
  bossiness in, 96–97
  bullying in, 95–96, 130
  designer clothing and, 78–79
  foul language in, 142
  making friends in, 94–95
  at parties, 89–90
  sharing in, 86–87, 95
  shyness in, 94–95
  tattling in, 70–71
  taunting in, 84–85, 95–96, 110–111
  teasing in, 95–96, 103–104, 205
  *see also* play behavior
perfectionism, 22, 155–156
play behavior, 80–81, 83–84, 86–87
  sex play in, 147–148
poker chip incentive system, 36, 175
pornography, 145–147
positive vs. negative statements, 25
power struggles, 31, 38, 43, 94
  at bedtime, 62
  over eating problems, 49–50
  in getting dressed, 58
  in toilet training, 50–51, 55–56
praise, 22–24, 26, 40
  conditional, 23
  of qualities vs. actions, 23
preschoolers, 27, 46, 77, 96, 144, 170
  touching of household objects by, 47–48, 207–208
privacy, 72, 140, 150, 194
  of body parts, 143–144, 147, 148
privileges, 25, 177
  denial of, 31–33, 128–129, 134, 137, 183, 185
  as incentive, 36–37, 131–133, 134
  of older sibling, 65–66, 161–162
professional counseling, 55, 72, 78, 86, 112, 122, 124–126, 133, 134, 145, 197–198, 201
property damage, 106–107, 171, 208–209
  touching of household objects and, 47–48, 207–208
protective reactions, parental, 205–210
  against false accusations, 205, 209
  problems with neighbors in, 208–209
  problems with teachers in, 206–207, 209
  religious proselytizing and, 210
  spanking by other adult in, 207–208
public masturbation, 140
public nudity, 142–143
punishment, 27

rebelliousness, 22, 25, 32, 38, 56, 90, 113, 132, 134, 156
regressive behavior, 51, 52, 68
reinforcement, behavioral, 36, 46, 52, 60, 61, 70, 86, 105, 131, 141, 176
religious proselytizing, 210
REM sleep, 153
restaurants, inappropriate behavior in, 82–83
revenge, threats of, 186–187
role playing, 89, 96, 101
rudeness, 73–74, 79–80, 84–86
rules, *see* discipline; limits, setting of
running away, 182–183
  from home, threat of, 187–188

school problems, 115–137, 166, 168, 185, 188
  aggressive behavior, 130–133
  attendance, 120–122

caused by teachers, 206–207, 209
cheating, 128–130
of late bloomers, 134–135
learning problems, 124–126, 206
motivation problems, 126–127, 134–135
paying attention, 124–126
separation anxiety, 117–118
stress-induced physical symptoms, 119–120, 207
suspension for, 136–137
teacher-parent communication about, 101–102, 127, 131–133, 135–136
underachievement, 133–135
*see also* homework
secrets, family, 191, 194–195
security, sense of, 22, 28, 44, 172
self-abuse, 111–112
self-esteem, 22, 23, 34, 54, 70, 79, 110, 116, 178
fears and, 167–168
self-image, 115
sensitivity to feelings, 73–74, 79–80, 84–86, 110–111
separation anxiety, 21
in school problems, 117–118
over visitation after divorce, 201–203
sex play, 147–148
sexual abuse, 52, 126, 147–148
sexual activity, parental, 60, 62, 149–150
sexual fantasies, 143
sexual issues, 139–150, 163–164
foul language, 141–142
gender identification, 144–145
inappropriate touching, 148
parental sexual activity, 60, 62, 149–150
sex play, 147–148
sexually oriented magazines, 145–147
*see also* genitalia; nudity
sharing, 95
with siblings, 86–87
shyness, 93–95
in peer relationships, 94–95
talking and, 93–94
in team sports, 166–167
sibling rivalry, 65–66, 97–98
"special time" and, 98
siblings, 74, 194–195
aggressive behavior among, 35, 108–110
fairness and, 160–161
jealousy of, 159–162
older, 65–66, 161–162
sharing with, 86–87
tattling on, 70
silliness, 30, 90–91, 183
sleep, 27, 46–47, 52, 207
in parents' bed, 156–157
REM, 153
smoking, 195
social behavior, 69–98, 168
acceptance of personal accountability in, 74–75
imaginary playmates in, 72
other people's reaction to, 69
in restaurants, 82–83
sensitivity to others' feelings and, 73–74, 79–80, 84–86, 110–111
silliness in, 30, 90–91, 183
stealing in, 71, 77–78, 209
toward strangers, 88–89
talking in, 92–94
while riding in cars, 75–76
*see also* inappropriate remarks; peer relationships; sportsmanship
social skills groups, 111
soiling, purposeful, 51, 54–56
spanking, 27–28
by child-care person, 67–68
by other adult, 207–208
"special time," 98
sports, team, 71, 91–92, 166–167
sportsmanship, 71, 81
being first vs., 91–92
cheating vs., 83–84
stealing, 71, 77–78, 209
strangers, overfriendliness toward, 88–89
stress, 29, 153
physical symptoms induced by, 119–120, 207
substance abuse, 126
alcohol in, 191, 194–195, 197–198
smoking in, 195
suicide, threats of, 188–189
suspension from school, 136–137

talent, inadequate, 164–165
talking, 24–25, 40, 83, 85
chattering, 92–93
shyness vs., 93–94
in social behavior, 92–94
tantrums, 30, 34, 63, 104–105, 175
tattling, 70–71, 197
taunting, 84–85, 95–96, 110–111
teacher-parent communication, 101–102, 127, 131–133, 135–136
teachers, problems with, 206–207, 209
team sports, 71, 91–92, 166–167
teasing, 95–96, 103–104, 205
"terrible twos," 50–51, 181
testing of limits, 21, 43–44, 49, 61
threats, 181–189
of revenge, 186–187
of running away from home, 187–188
of suicide, 188–189
*see also* challenges

time limits, 30, 31–32, 39, 57, 60, 127–128, 170
time-outs, 25, 28–30, 31, 37, 47, 90–91, 96–97, 103, 104–105, 141, 177, 183
  appropriate situations for, 29–30
  chain lock on room door for, 170–171
  oppositional behavior and, 169–172
toilet training, 50–51
  purposeful soiling and, 51, 54–56
touching:
  of genitalia, 140, 147, 148, 164
  of household objects by preschoolers, 47–48, 207–208
  inappropriate, 148
  negative, 27
  *see also* affection, physical
trust, 192
  broken by lying, 128, 179, 209
tuning out, 172–173
turn taking, 65, 97

underachievement, school, 133–135
unloving attitude, parents accused of, 185–186

verbal abuse, 39, 193
visitation after divorce, 201–203

whining, 30, 35, 174–175
"Who cares?," 185

yelling, 25–26, 37, 61, 124
  by teachers, 207
"You can't make me!," 183–184
"You don't love me!," 185–186
"You'll be sorry!," 186–187